INCREDIBLE LIFE
Of
TONTO KOWALSKI

THIS BOOK WILL ADD QUALITY YEARS TO YOUR LIFE!

THOMAS EDWARD MUSER
MASTER TRAINER
NSCA—CPT
NASM—CPT

Copyright © 2015 Thomas Edward Muser
All rights reserved.

Cover, exercise and Indian photos by Dawn Kingston

ISBN: 1502814056
ISBN 13: 9781502814050
Library of Congress Control Number: 2014918867
CreateSpace Independent Publishing Platform
North Charleston, South Carolina

This book is dedicated to:

Carol Ann Muser
and
William Edward Muser II

My terrific parents!

Endorsement

Open and honestly, Mr. Muser has created a valuable and entertaining "how-to" on achieving true success in life.

It's not a blueprint for making you shine in the eyes of others. Instead, he shows us that by doing the right things, and living life to the fullest, all of us can master our own destinies.

By reaching our own highest standards in what truly matters, life becomes its own incredible reward.

—Geoff Brehob, Real Estate Specialist

Contents

Introduction ix
Purpose xiii

Chapter 1 – Three Simple Rules 1
Chapter 2 – Setting Goals 12
Chapter 3 – Planning Your Day.. 21
Chapter 4 – Self-Discipline 27
Chapter 5 – What Drives Successful People?....................... 34
Chapter 6 – Exercise... 39
Chapter 7 – Nutrition.. 49
Chapter 8 – Attitude Can Shift All Things in Your Favor 61
Chapter 9 – Money.. 67
Chapter 10 – Investing and Saving.. 76
Chapter 11 – Equity and Debt.. 85
Chapter 12 – Frugality.. 90
Chapter 13 – Family 96
Chapter 14 – The Importance of a Strong Work Ethic 99
Chapter 15 – The Energizer Bunny... 104
Chapter 16 – Friends 112
Chapter 17 – My Favorite Motivators and Role Models...... 115
Chapter 18 – Faith in God.. 120
Chapter 19 – Mission Statement: Purpose in Life 125
Chapter 20 – Travel! See the World—It's Beautiful.............. 128
Chapter 21 – Mistakes and Decision-Making 133
Chapter 22 – The Value and Importance of Time 149
Chapter 23 – What Makes a Great Personal Trainer?......... 156

Chapter 24 – The Game of Life 164
Chapter 25 – Summary 170
Chapter 26 – About the Author 176
        a. The College Years 180
        b. My Bartending Career/Hobby 184
        c. My Manufacturing/Engineering/
           Production Career 192
        d. My Personal Training Career 203
Chapter 27 – Deleted Scenes 219
Two in the Loft 221
A $3,500 Night 223
Testimonials 226
Appendix A Sample weekly shopping list 230
Appendix B Shopping list broken down by nutrients 232
Appendix C Example monthly budget tracking 234
Resources and Recommended Learning Tools 238
Author Biography 241

Introduction

As I drove to the airport, I felt nervous and excited. I was flying from Boston to San Diego on a 7:00 a.m. flight. I was anxious because for the past two weeks, the news had been fixated on the Malaysian plane that vanished without a trace. I also thought of the plane bound from Boston to California that crashed into the World Trade Center. I was excited because I had never been to San Diego, and I always wanted to go. I had heard fantastic stories about the weather, the girls, and the city.

As I boarded the plane with my small carry-on, I looked for my reserved window seat. People told me it would be a great view of the city just before landing. My bag was filled with just the necessities: tank tops, shorts, flip-flops, my itinerary, a guidebook for the city, protein bars, and a camera. I stuffed it into the overhead bin, and then I slid into my window seat.

Just then, I looked up and saw a beautiful blond girl coming down the aisle. I could tell by her sculptured physique that she took great care of her body. I looked up toward the sky and said, "Please, God, may she have the seat right next to me!" He came close; she sat in the same row on the other side of the plane. Now my prayers switched: "Please, God, may no one sit between us!" This he answered. She gave me a smile and acknowledged me before reaching into her carry-on bag. She took out a book and began to read.

An hour and half went by, and she never looked up. She was just so into that book. I could tell by the way she squirmed in her seat and giggled at times that she was really enjoying her reading. Finally, I thought, *What the heck? Go ask her what's so great about the book.* So I got up and slid on over to her and said, "Excuse me, I just couldn't help noticing how into that book you are. Would you mind telling me what's it about?"

She looked a little startled by my question. She hesitated and then replied, "Well, this is a little embarrassing. But I'll tell you—it's about penises."

I just said, "Wow," because that caught me off guard.

She kept going. "Yes, it's really very interesting. Like, did you know an American Indian had the longest one ever recorded? And a Polish man's had the largest diameter."

I replied, "No, I wasn't aware of those facts. You are really quite interesting. What is your name?"

She replied, "Susan. What's yours?"

I said, "Susan, it is a real pleasure to meet you. My name is Tonto Kowalski."

This was a joke I'd heard when I was in my twenties. I had been sitting next to my friend Mark, and he'd just started cracking up out of the blue. I asked, "What the heck is so funny?"

He said, "I was just thinking of a joke a someone told me." I said, "Let me hear that joke!" For some reason, I never forgot it.

I did recently take a trip to San Diego for a fitness conference, but unfortunately there was no gorgeous blonde sitting on the plane with

INTRODUCTION

me. There were plenty in San Diego! I included that joke, which I do not take credit for, to explain where the Tonto name originated from.

I liked the name and refer to "Tonto" as my inner voice. He is the one who will pop up on my shoulder and tell me the right thing to do. I believe that everybody has this inner voice, and it's important to listen to him or her at certain times. For me, it is Tonto. For you, it might be someone different. If you are female, it might even be Pocahontas.

It is funny, but I first noticed this concept in the movie *Animal House*. A young man has two figures pop up on his shoulders: an angel and a devil. The devil suggests one action, and the angel gives him another. The angel tells him the right thing to do!

This book is about doing the right thing. Tonto is a good guy; he has your best interest in mind when he guides you. He understands your goals and why they're important to you. He knows your skills, talents, and purpose in life. He knows which tasks you need to do daily to reach your goals. I want each of you to find your own Tonto!

Purpose

This book contains humorous stories of people and real-life situations that will teach you valuable life lessons. The objective is for you to apply many of the suggestions and recommendations to your own life. The improvements will benefit you, your family, and all the people around you.

The information in this book has the potential to bring about positive lifestyle changes that could add many quality years to your life.

In the past few years, I have attended wakes and funerals for people I grew up with and/or went to high school or college with. This is alarming; fifty years old is too young to leave this world. If you could add quality years to your life, wouldn't you like that?

A few years ago, I wrote my personal mission statement: I was put on this great Planet Earth to help people improve the quality of their lives through fitness. I have added to this statement because I have learned that I can also help people with nutritional advice, motivation, encouragement, education, and suggested lifestyle changes.

Currently, I work full time as a personal trainer and part time as a bartender. You might say that in one job, I put calories in, and in the other job, I take them out. One profession supports the other. I have learned a lot from dealing with people in both professions. I have seen people change for the good and for the bad. My goal is to share with you some important discoveries and findings that you can utilize to make smart decisions in your life.

Prior to working as a personal trainer, which I have been doing for around ten years, I worked in the manufacturing and production field for eighteen years. My college degree is in industrial technology, which involves improving existing processes, reducing wasted steps, and finding the most efficient ways to accomplish tasks. Many of the principles I learned in the production world can be applied to our daily lives to make things easier.

One client came up to me the other day, and I could tell from the tense look on his face and his frustrated, quick pace that something was wrong. I just looked at him, and before I could say anything, he said, "I need to simplify my life. It's just too complicated!" I had another client say to me the week before, "I feel like a piece of human taffy being pulled in all directions!"

Sometimes, we do need to step back and look at our lives. Discovering ways to make life less complicated reduces stress and allows us to concentrate on things we enjoy more and are important to us. In this book, you will learn how to prioritize your day, set goals, and accomplish what you were meant to achieve, which will bring you the greatest satisfaction. We only play this game of life once; we might as well win it by utilizing all the skills, talents, and gifts that we have been given!

Chapter 1 – Three Simple Rules

In my life, I have found that when I do these three things every day, everything else in life seems to fall right into place:

    1. Get enough sleep (seven to eight hours)

    2. Work out (both strength and cardio)

    3. Eat right (four to six balanced meals per day)

By doing these three things, you put yourself in a great position to accomplish the goals you set for yourself. Following this routine allows you to maintain a healthy, positive attitude and keeps your energy level up where it needs to be.

If any one of the three items is missing, it can easily snowball, and you will lose the others. If you don't get enough sleep, you could be too tired to work out. If you don't work out, that could throw off your eating plan. It you are not eating right, you might not have the right energy for your workout.

When I was in my twenties, I worked a third-shift job, 11:00 p.m. to 7:00 a.m., for about three years. This job made me realize how important sleep is. If you have ever worked a third-shift job or you are currently working the third shift, you know how it can screw up your sleeping routine. You can almost go back to a normal routine on your days off, but then you have to adjust and try to get some good sleep during the day before you go back to work. That first day back can be very tough. Constantly changing your sleep routine will result in days when you just don't feel like working out or doing other important tasks.

If you look back on your life and think about the times you were most productive and happy, chances are, you were doing these three things daily.

Things do happen in life that can prevent you from accomplishing these three things on a daily basis. For example, a newborn baby might not allow you to sleep through the night. And that's all cool; those things take a higher priority. As long as you are aware of it, however, if there are not good reasons for missing the three daily items, it makes sense to make them a priority.

Working out helps you get a good night's sleep. I have been running a small-group training class on Monday nights at 5:30 p.m. It's a great class that uses kettle bells, total-body resistance exercises (TRX), Total Gym, and other fun pieces of equipment. The class has five or six stations, and we'll do circuit training for two- or three-minute intervals for an hour. One of the participants told me he always sleeps well on Monday nights because of this workout.

One of the reasons these three things are the key to high performance is that together, they allow your mind (your brain) to operate efficiently.

The mind/brain is the most complex and complicated part of our bodies. Some people ask whether the brain is an organ or a muscle. It is an organ; however, I believe it behaves like a muscle in its relationship to the use-it-or-lose-it principle. When you don't use certain muscles, atrophy sets in, and they lose size and strength. When you don't use parts of your brain, I believe the same thing happens.

Chapter 1 – Three Simple Rules

My dad went to the gym three days a week when he was in his seventies. One day, he went to the gym and found it had closed. He stopped working out. I knew this wasn't good for him; he really enjoyed his workout routine. I took him to a few other gyms in the area, but he just wasn't interested. The gym that had closed was right across the street from him; he used to walk there. About six months after he stopped working out, his memory started to go. He couldn't remember if he had paid his bills or not, and he couldn't balance his checkbook. Soon, my brother Danny had to take over paying his bills. We didn't realize this at the time, but these were the first stages of dementia. My dad is now in a nursing home. He has been diagnosed with dementia, and his short-term memory is nowhere close to what it used to be. I will visit him at 7:00 p.m. and ask him what he had for dinner at 5:30 p.m. Not only will he not remember what he had for dinner, but he won't even know whether he ate or not.

Now, I share this with you for an important reason: I am truly convinced that by exercising, eating right, and getting enough sleep, you can add good, quality years to your life. I also believe that by doing these things daily, you will reduce the risk of dementia, Alzheimer's, heart disease, and cancer. Some of you might just agree with what I am saying simply because you've read it in magazines or books or have heard it on TV. Others might ask for scientific facts and studies to back up what I am saying.

Cardiff University published the results of a thirty-five-year study on December 9, 2013. Monitoring the health habits of 2,235 men over a thirty-five-year period confirmed that exercise significantly reduces the risk of dementia. The study is the longest of its kind to probe the influence of environmental factors in chronic disease. (Source: www.sciencedaily.com)

Doing exercise every day can considerably reduce your risk of developing Alzheimer's disease. Even becoming physically active after eighty years of age helps reduce risk, as researchers from Rush University Medical Center have reported in the journal *Neurology*. (Source: www.medicalnewstoday.com)

Train your brain by challenging it to do things it has never done before. Learn a new language or a new skill, or write a book (like I am doing right now). Train your neuromuscular system, which is the combination of your nervous system and your muscular system working together to produce movement.

The brain is the center of the nervous system, and most decisions and movements we choose to make have to go through the brain. When we decide to move in a certain way, our brain sends signals through the nervous system to our muscles, which allow us to move. So if you pick up a couple of moderate-sized dumbbells, balance on one leg, and do an alternating shoulder press toward the sky, you are working your neuromuscular system. Your brain has to send many different signals to many different muscles for your body to perform this movement.

So, we can conclude that if our brains are not functioning at peak ability, we may make poor decisions. And at times, our movements might not be as smooth as we'd like them to be.

That brings us back to our three simple rules:

- Sleep: The mind works best when it is well rested!

- Food: The brain primarily runs off glucose, which comes from food!

- Exercise: Training the neuromuscular system can create new nerve endings in the brain, which allows it to store more data.

Chapter 1 – Three Simple Rules

Exercise can even grow the brains of older adults, says researcher Kirk I. Erickson, PhD, assistant professor of psychology at the University of Pittsburgh. In his recent study, older adults without Alzheimer's, aged sixty to eighty, walked at a moderate pace for thirty to forty-five minutes three days a week for a year. The research showed that study participants had a 2 percent increase in the volume of their hippocampus, a region of the brain important for memory. He also found growth in another brain area important for memory—the prefrontal cortex. (Source: www.webmd.com)

Let's dig a little deeper and gather more information that proves these three things will help us perform better.

You know that if you don't get a good night's sleep, it can affect your performance the next day. Different people have different thoughts about sleep, and many researchers have done studies to determine how much sleep is the right amount. I believe it is not the same for everyone, but most people perform best when they get between six and a half to eight hours of sleep. Seven and a half hours works best for me.

I have a friend who sleeps only four to five hours a night, and he still has tons of energy during the day and is highly successful. He meditates for twenty minutes every day. He feels that the twenty minutes of transcendental meditation is equal to four hours of sleep. Based on my friend's performance, I believe it. Jerry Seinfeld, who has been doing transcendental meditation for over forty years, refers to it as a battery charger for your brain.

As I mentioned earlier, proper nutrition, along with a tailored exercise program, will allow you to optimize your sleep and get good quality sleep.

Next, food! How does the brain run? What fuels the brain? Have you ever been so hungry that you just can't think straight? That has happened to me. I was at the gym and had just gotten through training four clients in a row, and I was on my way to eat. A woman came up to me and started asking me questions about triathlon training. I remember her talking to me, but I just wasn't registering what she was saying. I said to myself, *Tom, you just can't answer this person intelligently. All you keep thinking about is food. You haven't eaten in four hours, and you are out of fuel. Go and get something to eat!* So I said to her, "Hold that thought. I need to take care of an important task. Can I meet you right back here in thirty minutes?"

She said, "I'll be over on the treadmill."

I said, "Great, I will come and find you." As I was eating, my mind started to clear, and I could formulate the best responses to her questions.

Sometimes in this situation, I simply say to the individual, "My blood-sugar level is dropping, and my glycogen stores are depleted. I need fifteen minutes to refuel." Based on what they do or don't know about of glycogen and blood sugar, some look at me strangely, as though they think I must have some sort of serious medical condition. No, numb-nuts, I'm just friggin' hungry! What's important is not letting yourself get to the point where you're starving and not thinking straight. That's when overeating and making bad food choices come easy.

Most research shows that the brain primary runs off glucose, which comes from carbohydrates. However, if I am starving, not thinking straight, and out of fuel, I eat half of a small, whole chicken and a few handfuls of almonds, and I am good to go, no doubt about it! Actually, that sounds pretty good right now! Chicken and almonds are primarily protein and fats, not carbohydrates, but I know they will help me think more clearly. The term *gluconeogenesis* explains how glucose comes from noncarbohydrates, but I don't want to get all technical on you.

Chapter 1 – Three Simple Rules

Other times when I was extremely hungry and not thinking clearly, I ate a banana and sharpened right up. Bananas digest quickly into glucose molecules, getting into the bloodstream and to the brain very rapidly.

The difference between these two scenarios is that the banana will last about an hour and a half, while the chicken and almonds will last three to four hours. Ideally, both together offer a longer source of good fuel for the brain and the rest of the body.

When I work a four-hour shift bartending at the restaurant or train four clients in a row at the gym, that's too long for me to go without eating and sustain the energy level I want. So I always bring a small snack to eat halfway through, such as a banana or a small bag of almonds or cashews. Both places of employment tend to have attractive women there, and it is not uncommon for one of them to see me carrying in these items. My corny response is usually: "Why are you staring at my banana?" Or "Why are you looking at my nuts?" Sorry, HR (human resources), it's all in good fun. A sense of humor is important for a great work environment.

When you go the gas pump, you select the type of fuel you want for your vehicle. You have choices: regular, plus, super, and premium. Some gas stations have three choices, and some have four.

I think of food like these choices. When we put better fuel in our bodies, they run better and are less likely to break down on us. When you run out of fuel in your car, it can't run. If you put in too much fuel, the tank overflows, the engine floods, or you blow up the gas station. Maybe an explosion is taking the metaphor too far. But think of a high school reunion when you might have said to your friend, "Look at So-and-So! Hasn't he just blown up?" So maybe my explosion theory isn't too far off. Your tank is only built for so much fuel at a time. You can't put thirty gallons into an eighteen-gallon tank without some type of consequence.

So put in the right amount, roughly between four hundred and six hundred calories per meal. Adjust according to your fitness goals. And make sure it is premium fuel. A premium meal consists of a vegetable, a whole-grain product or starchy carbohydrate, and a good protein.

Some of my favorite meals are as follows:

- Six ounces of baked chicken breast, one cup brown rice, and one cup broccoli

- Eight ounces of baked haddock, one large spinach salad with tomatoes

- Six ounces of top round steak, one medium sweet potato, one cup string beans

- One apple, two rice cakes, and twenty almonds

- One turkey sandwich on whole wheat bread with lettuce and tomato

These provide good fuel for your brain and your body! There will be more information on nutrition later in the book.

I don't want to bore you by listing numerous research studies concluding that exercise, eating right, and getting enough rest will reduce your risk of many life-threatening and life-altering diseases. I could fill a library with that stuff. By doing these three things regularly, your body and brain will run at peak performance.

Chapter 1 – Three Simple Rules

The most important point about these three simple rules is this: you are in absolute control of the three items. You control what goes into your mouth, you can choose to do some type of workout every day, and you can choose what time to go to bed!

In life, we encounter so many things that we have no authority over. Things happen at our jobs that we cannot control. Customers and clients relocate, orders get canceled, companies get bought out, new management is hired, factories shut down and relocate or consolidate, and restaurants and stores go out of business. All these types of things happen to us, and we have no control over most of them. But we are in charge of how we react to these situations.

We do have control over our exercising, eating well-balanced meals, and getting enough rest. And by doing these three things, other stressful situations will not seem as bad.

I had a fantastic workout today, and all I keep thinking about is tomorrow's workout. You can and will become addicted to working out. When I have fantastic workouts, everything else in life gets reduced to the proper size. I don't worry about my jobs or financial problems. I know that if I get my workouts in, eat right, and get enough rest, I will be able to handle any situation that comes along. And so will you. It's that simple.

So, how do you get started? How do you make sure these three items are your normal, everyday lifestyle from here on in? It depends on what level you are at. Everyone gets some sleep, eats, and does some type of activity (even if it is just walking to the car). As you read through the above material, something likely jumped out at you, and a little Tonto popped up off your shoulder and whispered in your ear, "You know, you could be doing a better job in this area!"

Small Steps

The key is small steps; you do not have to change everything at once. Perhaps you have been skipping breakfast. Starting next week, you could start each day with a sensible breakfast: a banana, a bowl of Total raisin bran with skim milk, and an eight-ounce glass of orange juice. Is that the best breakfast in the world for you? It might not be, but it is better than nothing. I could say to start off with an egg-white omelet filled with fresh veggies like peppers and mushrooms, one slice of whole wheat toast without butter, and a glass of water. Your response might be, "I don't have time to make an omelet in the morning," or "I hate egg whites and veggies." The key is to start with something you like and fit meal preparation into your daily routine.

Now, let's take exercise. I have had so many people say to me, "I just hate exercising. I find it extremely boring. Is there any way you could make it fun?" I love hearing this, because absolutely, you can make it fun! Now, I must interject here—I have numerous clients tell me that they do not share the same definition of *fun* that I do. As a matter of fact, if I say to one of my clients, "Come on! Ready to have some fun?" He replies, "Fun—are we going out for pizza and beer?"

There are many ways to exercise. The trick is to find resistance training exercises and cardiovascular exercises that you enjoy doing and that feel effective. If you don't have any type of cardiovascular exercise in your weekly routine, you could start with walking for thirty minutes, three days a week. If you have stairs at your workplace or where you live, you could start with walking up ten flights of stairs. The next time you do it, walk up eleven flights, and then do twelve. With resistance training, start with some push-ups, sit-ups, and holding in a plank position for thirty seconds. It might be three push-ups, ten sit-ups, and twenty seconds with the plank. That's OK! You are just starting off. And like I tell a lot of new clients, lifting a twelve-ounce beer can or

Chapter 1 — Three Simple Rules

eight-ounce wine glass from the table to your mouth does not qualify as resistance training.

If you realize that you have not been getting enough good, quality sleep, start tonight. Set a specific time to get into bed. If this is a new time for you, you might not fall asleep right away. That's OK. Get up at your desired time, and then make sure you eat right and exercise during the day. That night, you will fall asleep quicker. It could even take a few days or a week for your body to adjust to your new lifestyle.

There will be more on exercise and nutrition in later chapters. The key is to start with something! Start with small steps!

Chapter 2 – Setting Goals

My first Cape Cod Beach House!

The power of goal setting is amazing! I first learned this in my thirties. I set ten aggressive goals for myself at the beginning of the year. At the end of the year, I was amazed that I had accomplished nine out of the ten goals. One of those goals was to purchase a beach house in Cape Cod, Massachusetts. Another was to earn $125,000 per year. I achieved both. These were very challenging goals, and I felt tremendous satisfaction upon completion.

Financial goals are important, and a higher wage or salary is something most people will shoot for. When I hit my $125,000-per-year goal, I was excited and pleasantly surprised. So, the following year, I said, "What the heck? If this setting-goals thing works, I'll go for a hundred

Chapter 2 – Setting Goals

and fifty thousand per year." This 20 percent improvement was a pretty aggressive goal. I didn't reach it; I ended up with $146,000 per year, which was not bad, a 17 percent increase. When I decided to leave the engineering/manufacturing world, become a personal trainer, and make a career in the fitness industry, this was a different type of goal. I knew I was going to take a substantial pay cut. I was OK with that. I realized that money isn't everything and that I needed only so much to live comfortably and be happy. I also had a deep thought in the back of my mind. It was Tonto talking. He said, "Hey, Tom, if you were that successful in a field you're not really passionate about, how much success will you experience and how many people will you help in a field that you feel incredibly passionate about?"

Happiness is something a lot of people strive for. One of the remarkable things I learned about setting goals is that happiness is the end result. In addition to feeling happy when you achieve your goals, you also feel contentment when you are doing tasks that move you toward achieving those goals. I recall being ridiculously happy when I was driving down to the Cape to look at some properties. I had not bought my Cape beach house yet, but I knew I was getting close. I had six houses lined up to look at with a real estate agent, and I was as excited as a kid on Christmas morning. I had put in lots of work to get me to this point: I had researched the market and worked with the agent to line up the right properties. Sure enough, I bought one of those houses.

You can set all types of goals: long term, yearly, monthly, and daily. Goals can be financial, tangible, spiritual, or family related; they can be places to visit, education to obtain, fun trips, and so on. A goal should make you excited when you think about it.

Courses and books on setting goals will state that you should have goals in four areas of your life: family, career, financial, and health. I would like to add spiritual, educational, and pleasure.

A Harvard University study surveyed a class of students on goals. They found that ten years later, the 2 percent of people who had written goals had a higher net worth than the other 98 percent combined. Now, that's an amazing statistic!

So start today if you haven't already. Grab a piece of paper or your computer and write down ten aggressive, challenging, and worthwhile goals that you want to achieve in the next year. If now is not your peak-performance time, then schedule a time this week to sit down and write your goals. I believe we all have a peak-performance time during the day when our minds are the sharpest. For me, it is around 9:30 a.m., provided I worked out the previous day, got a good night's sleep, and stuck to my nutrition plan. After a good, nutritious breakfast and nice cup of Starbucks dark espresso roast, I feel like I could solve any problem, deal with any issue, or tackle any task or event.

The more detailed your goals are, the higher probability you have to achieve them. For example, if you add a start time and completion date, that will help. Writing down the necessary steps to achieve each goal is even better. The management courses I have attended always use the acronym SMART when referring to setting goals. Your goals should be: Specific, Measurable, Attainable, Relevant, and Time-bound. So make sure your goals are SMART!

Defining your goals should take you no more than thirty minutes. In half an hour, you will figure out 95 percent of the goals you would really like to achieve. I like to do this on a yearly basis. But don't wait till January 1 to write them. Whatever month you are in, write goals for the next twelve months. On January 1, you can revisit them and then modify and add to them to fill up the rest of the year.

This is exciting! At the end of the year, you get to rate yourself. Give yourself a grade on how you did the previous year, and then get psyched for the upcoming year. Time to set new goals!

Chapter 2 – Setting Goals

I currently have ten goals, and one time-bound goal is to finish this book by the end of the year. Most of my other goals are not financial. Do you want to know what they are? Ah, what the heck—here is my list:

1. Visit my dad at Life Care (a nursing home) a minimum of once per week (ongoing).

2. Maintain and improve family relations: attend birthdays and other events, send cards, and make calls (ongoing).

3. Eat right daily and keep learning about nutrition (forever).

4. Train hard every day and keep learning about how the human body works (forever).

5. Finish writing my book by the end of the year.

6. Sell my Saint Joseph Street property and clean and maintain my other properties.

7. Practice frugality and reduce debt wherever possible—the goal is to be debt free by age fifty-five.

8. Perform thirty personal training sessions per week.

9. Attend church a minimum of once per week (ongoing).

10. Take time to enjoy life's simple treasures—mountain climbing, biking, kayaking, fishing, and traveling.

This list of goals is not in any type of order. I rewrite them every morning to reinforce their importance and keep them fresh in my mind.

When you rewrite or reread your goals, it makes you feel good! There is a scientific explanation for this: writing your goals, rewriting them, and reading them often will release the chemical dopamine, a feel-good endorphin! In Loretta Graziano Breuning's book, *Meet Your Happy Chemicals: Dopamine, Endorphin, Oxytocin, Serotonin*, she writes how happiness is a surge of these chemicals. She explains that dopamine triggers a good feeling when you approach a reward. Achieving your goal is your reward. The deeper you research this, the bigger scientific terms you will have. You can trace all this back to certain parts of the brain, but you don't need to get that technical. Just know that thinking about your goals and working on them will make you feel great!

Forget about depression medication or feeling down at times. Think about and work on your goals!

Who do you share your goals with? That's a great question! You share them with people who will also be excited about you achieving them and people who can help you achieve some of your goals. Share your goals with people who will motivate you and even put some pressure on you to keep you on track. Share them with people to motivate them and inspire them to also pursue goals and be better people.

I have shared my goal of writing this book with more people than any other goal I have ever set for myself. The more people I tell, the more pressure I put on myself to complete it. I like it when people ask me, "How is the book coming along?" When I see these people next year, I am not going to say, "Still working on it," or "I changed my mind and decided not to finish it." My reply will be, "I finished it, and I think it came out awesome."

Chapter 2 – Setting Goals

Long-term goals are also very important. I will share with you some of my long-term goals.

1. Build a log cabin or similar house on our family's land in the White Mountains, New Hampshire, with no mortgage within three years.

2. Pay off my West Hyannisport, Massachusetts, house in the next ten years.

3. Live in Fort Lauderdale, Florida during the winter months and Cape Cod, Massachusetts, and the White Mountains, New Hampshire, in the summer months at age fifty-five.

4. At age sixty-five, I won't have to work unless I decide to. I will have enough money coming in monthly from my investments so I can live the way I want to live.

When setting a goal, I believe it is really important to know why that goal is important to you. My first long-term goal is important to me because, many years ago, my grandmother told my grandfather that he needed to buy land up in the White Mountains of New Hampshire so that their kids (my dad and his sister) would have a place to spend their summers. She did not want them spending their summers in the city. So my grandfather bought the land, and my dad and his sister spent the summers up in the mountains. Sure enough, my parents did the same thing with us kids; my brothers, sister, and I spent our summers up in the White Mountains. I'll always remember going to the barber and getting our heads buzzed before the trip. All us boys got the very short crew cut (for low-maintenance reasons, I believe). I did not think it was fair that my sister did not get the same haircut! So, my family has some terrific memories from that land. Also, my grandparents and my mom are buried up there, a short walk from the property, on a beautiful mountainside. So, to have a sweet log cabin on that land where we can enjoy one of life's treasures (the White Mountains of New Hampshire), visit my mom and grandparents, and reminisce about fun days growing up just makes sense to me. This goal truly excites me when I think about it.

Now, let's take a look at my second goal and how it will be achieved. This can be broken down mathematically and tracked on a monthly basis. I have ten years to get this accomplished; I owe $230,000 on the house. So that is $23,000 per year, which breaks down to $1,917 per month that I have to pay on the principal. Not an easy goal! Currently, I am paying $415 per month on the principal. I don't have an extra $1,502 each month right now to put toward the goal. However, just thinking about it, I feel my mind start to work. *OK. Let me think of different ways to earn that type of money. I have three months to figure this out.* Then Tonto will pop up on my shoulder and say something like, "What if your life depended on it? Would you find a way to earn an additional fifteen hundred per month?" This goal is important to me because I believe that spending some quality time in a beautiful home that I own outright, not having to ever worry about making a mortgage payment again, will produce a rewarding feeling, a nice sense of accomplishment!

And never get discouraged by not achieving a goal. Look at it as a good thing; it is better to strive for something great and not get it than to not strive for it at all. It also means that you were nice and aggressive with setting goals. Too many people set their goals too low!

Chapter 2 – Setting Goals

*A goal is not always meant to be reached.
It often serves simply as something to aim at.*

—Bruce Lee

Once you develop the habit of setting goals, working on your goals, and achieving them, you will have that habit forever! It is like a fantastic drug that's addicting—but also legal and free.

I already have three goals for next year that I can't wait to work on! I am so excited about them! I have disciplined myself to finish this book prior to starting those goals. It actually puts a little pressure on me to get this book done so I can start working toward my new goals.

Do you want to hear them? What the heck, I'm sharing everything else with you.

1. Make three exercise videos.

2. Create and develop my own website.

3. Turn this book into an audio program.

If you recall, I wrote in the introduction of this book my mission statement: I was put on this great Planet Earth to help people improve the quality of their lives through fitness, motivation, education, and nutritional advice. These three goals really excite me because they will drastically increase the number of people I can reach and help.

Thomas Edward Muser

> Goals are not only absolutely necessary to motivate us.
> They are essential to really keep us alive!
>
> —Robert Schuller

Now you are ready to write down your goals! As Rocky said to Clubber Lang in *Rocky III*, "Go for it!"

Chapter 3 – Planning Your Day

In my manufacturing career, I attended several management courses that covered the five *P*s of success: Proper Planning Prevents Poor Performance. Some books list it as the six *P*s and throw the word *Prior* in there. I think that's just silly. When else are you going to plan? After you do the job? The British army uses the seven *P*s: Proper Planning and Preparation Prevents Piss-Poor Performance.

The five to ten minutes it takes for you to write down your daily tasks and plan your day can actually save hours of time by making you more efficient and productive. These minutes spent planning have the largest return on investment (ROI) that I can think of in regard to time and productivity. According to Brian Tracy (and I agree with him), taking about ten minutes to plan out your day could save up to two hours in wasted time and diffuse effort throughout the day.

When I first started getting busy as a personal trainer, my schedule filled up. One day, two clients showed up at the same time to train with me. This was my fault; I had double-booked myself. If you are in a similar line of work and you have done this, you know it sucks! I made the best of the situation and promised myself that it would never happen again. And, knock on wood, it hasn't! I plan my day, my week, and the following week with an electronic scheduler (cell phone and laptop) and have an appointment book where I manually write in all my appointments. Several times during the day, I match these up to make sure there are no double-bookings and that I have sufficient time to deliver an exception personal training session to each client.

When is the best time for you to plan your day? It can be done the night before or in the morning. I prefer planning in the morning, right after I have rewritten my yearly goals. Write down the seven most important things you need to do that day. You might have eight, nine, or more. I suggest you don't make your list too long; that could cause stress. But I do recommend at least seven items.

Next, take a few minutes to prioritize the items in the order in which they will be completed. As you complete them, you can check them off in a logical and efficient order.

Now it is very important to make sure the tasks you have written down for the day will move you toward the completion of your goals. If a task has absolutely nothing to do with your goals, you might want to take it off the list.

Many people review what they need to get done each day in their heads. Writing daily tasks down is more powerful. A great statistic I

Chapter 3 – Planning Your Day

heard at a time-management seminar is: when you write something down, you have a 50 percent better chance of remembering it, even if you don't read it again. So think about how that percentage increases when you read your tasks and goals a few times during the course of the day!

Some tasks can be as simple as food shopping, doing the laundry, mowing the lawn, and washing your car. Those are tasks that need to be done, and you should get credit for them.

Example of my daily task list:

- Eat right—five well-balanced meals that are low in sugar and saturated fat. Total calories: 2500. Total grams of protein: 175.

- Write for thirty minutes on my book.

- Work nine productive hours at the gym.

- Work out—thirty-five minutes upper-body strength, and twenty-five minutes cardio interval training.

- Drop off birthday present for niece.

- Shop for food—stick to budget: sixty-five dollars.

- Cook and prep food for tomorrow.

- Read for thirty minutes in my professional field.

I recommend having another daily list of prioritized tasks to accomplish at your office or place of employment. This will keep you on track. People at your office or workplace may ask you for help with something, or perhaps they just want to tell you about their weekend. These distractions can eat up time. By embedding your task list in the back of your mind, you will not allow certain distractions to prevent you from completing your tasks. If you don't plan your day, you can end up doing things that aren't related to your goals. You can get sidetracked very easily by whatever comes along and grabs your interest. And plenty of those things come along, whether you are at the office or at home. When you don't have an agenda of items to be completed, you are susceptible to all the temptations that life throws your way. For example, your buddy calls you up and says, "Hey, let's go hit a bucket of golf balls," or, "Let's go out for a bite to eat." If you really don't have a plan for the day, you say, "Why not?"

Some of these tasks can be social and fun. Tomorrow, one of my tasks is watching the New England Patriots from 8:30 p.m. to 11:30 p.m. with my brother, which I am very much looking forward to! Going to the beach, mountain climbing, fishing, and playing basketball are all examples of fun tasks.

Daily tasks can translate into accomplishing goals. For example, a good friend of mine married a very beautiful flight attendant. She had the prettiest smile and the whitest teeth I had ever seen. One day I asked her, "How do you keep your teeth so white?" She replied without hesitation, "I brush my teeth six times a day and floss them twice a day." She did not say, "I brush my teeth three, four, or five times a day and floss once or twice a day." Instead, she was very specific with her daily tasks. Her goal was clear: to have nice, white teeth. In her line of work, since she was meeting and serving people up close and personal, having white teeth was very important to her. She knew that when she stuck to her daily task of brushing and flossing, she would obtain her goal.

There will be days when completing your tasks is smooth and effortless. Some days, you might even do a few extra tasks related to

Chapter 3 – Planning Your Day

your goals that weren't on your list. And there will be days when some tasks take longer than expected and you won't complete them all. No worries! You will get them done the following day by adding them to your next daily list.

If losing weight is one of your current goals, what tasks should be on your daily list? Let me give you a little hint:

- Strength training (for example: thirty minutes of eight dumbbell exercises, three sets of each exercise with twelve repetitions per set)

- Cardiovascular work (for example: thirty-minute bike ride)

- Food shopping for the right nutrition

- Food preparation for the next day

If you need to lose weight and you perform these tasks on a daily basis, don't you think you would have a great chance of attaining your goal? Your nutrition plan might need to be fine-tuned to match your desired weight loss, and your strength and cardio work needs to be changed periodically to prevent boredom and keep your body from adapting to those eight exercises.

By planning your day and writing down the most important tasks you need to do that day, you give Tonto the ammunition he needs to keep you on track. You might get sluggish or lazy at one point in the day, and he'll pop up on your shoulder and say, "Hey, pal, stop wasting time and procrastinating. Get your next task done!"

At the end of the day, you get to reflect on how you did versus your daily task list. Looking back on the day, you get a great feeling when you have accomplished all the tasks on your list. A successful life is the result of many successful days put together. Planning your daily tasks allows you to sleep comfortably during the night and be excited about tomorrow. Your mind will work during the night to plan your next productive day!

> The victory of success is half won when one gains the habit of setting goals and achieving them. Even the most tedious chore will become endurable as you parade through each day convinced that every task, no matter how menial or boring, brings you closer to fulfilling your dreams.
>
> —Og Mandino

Chapter 4 – Self-Discipline

This is the best definition of self-discipline I have heard:

> Self-discipline is the ability to make yourself do what you should do, when you should do it, whether you feel like it or not.
>
> —Elbert Hubbard

Elbert Hubbard was a writer, artist, and philosopher who lived from 1856 to 1915, so self-discipline is not a new concept! Brian Tracy also uses this definition in many of his excellent programs.

I have done a lot of research on what it takes to achieve ultimate success. As I was investigating, one name came up a few times: Kop Kopmeyer. I read a little more about this man. He came up with one thousand success principles. His principles and findings, just plain and simple, make sense! He also concluded that making yourself do what you should do when you should do it, whether you feel like it or not, was the most important principle of all.

Being self-disciplined is so much easier said than done. Let me give you an example. Say that one of my goals is to stay in great physical shape. I have planned a thirty-minute strength-training routine with body-weight exercises followed by a two-mile walk on the beach. My buddy calls before I get out the door. He says, "Hey, I'm heading down to Lulu's on the beach for a burger and a beer. Come and join me!"

Even while I type this, I want the burger and the beer at Lulu's. The wait staff is always hot chicks not wearing much clothing. I know that if I work out first and meet him two hours later, though, I will accomplish two of my goals: staying in shape and maintaining friendships with some fun! I believe this type of control over emotions and impulses separates extremely successful people from the average. Remember, it's "whether you feel like it or not"!

Temptations to stray away from goals happen daily for everybody!

Here are some more examples:

You set up a great nutrition plan for yourself, which has limited sugars and no refined carbohydrates. Then there is a birthday party at the office with a big cake. You rationalize and say, "Hey, this person has worked for the company for thirty years; the least I can do is have a piece of cake with him."

The next morning, someone brings in a dozen donuts, and you say, "Wow, one will go great with my cup of coffee; I'll just work out a little harder at the gym today."

The temptations that come our way daily are actually the keys to our success! Think about it: the most successful people in the world do not let these temptations get them off track. They simply and politely say no. Why do they do this? Because they know that sticking to their plan, their goals, and their daily task list will give them the ultimate satisfaction they desire! One of Zig Ziglar's famous lines was: "You have to say no to the good so you can say yes to the best!"

Chapter 4 – Self-discipline

How many times have you done something or said something that you wished you could take back? I have, plenty of times! OK, Tonto says to be honest and tell the folks that most of those times involved alcohol. It's true, and I think many of us know that alcohol can contribute to making bad choices. As a bartender, it always impresses me when, after I've asked a group of people if they would like another round, one person responds, "I have reached my limit, my quota for the day. May I please have an ice water?" That person has the self-control and the self-discipline to make a logical decision despite pressure from others or the immediate gratification of having another beverage. Tonto might have given him a dope slap and said, "Hey, buddy, you know that if you have another drink, you will be over the legal limit for alcohol consumption. Be smart, have a couple of waters, and drive home safely."

People who do not have self-control and self-discipline don't know when they've had enough, and they usually get into some sort of trouble. Some trouble could be minor, like getting yelled at by a significant other for coming home late and drunk, or being late and unproductive at work the next day. Other trouble could be much worse, however, and we usually find out about it in the newspaper or see those accidents or events on TV.

Writing our goals and daily tasks each morning will absolutely help us avoid these situations and temptations! We will ask ourselves before we make these moves, "Is this right, and is this in line with our goals?"

Bottom line—you have the ability to set your goals and put together your daily tasks list related to your goals, and you have the self-discipline to stick to that plan.

One of my clients is preparing to run the London Marathon; this is an important goal he has set for himself. His daily tasks leading up to the marathon will include running a certain number of miles, strength training, and eating the right nutrition to support his training. It requires an incredible amount of self-discipline to complete these tasks on a daily basis while performing his full-time job and being there for his wife and kids. I fully believe that he will finish the race at his desired time. While he is training, he will be there for his family and do an excellent job at his place of employment. He works for a large London-based company, and I bet his coworkers and his boss will admire and appreciate his dedication and ability to balance those three important areas of his life.

Another client is competing in an all-natural body building show in three weeks. She has been preparing for this event for six months. When most people see a person, whether it's a guy or a girl, who is ripped and has an unbelievable muscular physique, they think that person is on steroids. They think these people must be on drugs—that's not healthy. It's not always true that they take drugs; I know many people with fantastic, sculpted bodies who have not used any. Instead, these people have a ridiculous amount of self-discipline. They put nothing into their bodies that could negatively affect their appearance. They train very hard—both in strength training and cardiovascular work. And the thrill of getting up on stage in front of hundreds of people to show off their hard work is highly satisfying and rewarding for them. Now, you might say, "That's all cool, and I am not going to that extreme to look better." That's OK. The trick is to have the self-discipline to balance your priorities and eat the foods and work out appropriately to obtain the physique that makes you most comfortable.

Setting goals, planning your day, and having the self-discipline to follow through and achieve the goals you set for yourself will become a positive and rewarding habit for you, which is really awesome. You will become addicted to it! As you approach the completion of your goal, you can see it within reach and you know you are going to get there, so you will start searching for your next goal to conquer. People experience a rush or a high while progressing toward the completion

Chapter 4 – Self-discipline

of their goals. I see it and hear it all the time; the two people I mentioned above are already talking about the next marathon, triathlon, or body building show.

Always remember, if you hold yourself responsible for your actions, and your actions are in line with your goals, you will have the best chance to achieve your goals!

Andrew Carnegie gave Napoleon Hill the task of interviewing five hundred millionaires across the country many years ago. These interviews took twenty years to complete and analyze. He concluded that these people had one thing in common: the ability to practice self-discipline! Successful people have the ability to make themselves do what they should do, when they should do it, whether they feel like it or not!

How do you develop this important skill? Think about the outcome; think about the goal being completed. You will need to do certain tasks and activities to reach those goals, and some days, you just won't feel like doing them. When you hit this point, that's when you place yourself head and shoulders above the competition. Look at those moments of discouragement as tests, and realize that self-discipline is what separates extremely successful people from average people.

Let me give you an example. Last week, I was leaving the gym around 9:30 p.m. I had trained ten people that day, all in one-hour sessions. I was mentally and physically exhausted, and I just wanted to go home, eat, and sleep. Something stopped me just before I got to the exit door, and Tonto popped up on my shoulder. He said, "Hey, Bozo, where the hell do you think you're going? You haven't worked out yet; you know very well that this morning you wrote down on your daily task list to train arms and core before you left the gym today! So turn your ass around, go back in the gym, and complete your workout!" I turned around and got the workout done. If I had not done that, it could have affected my sleep that night; I would have felt guilty for missing an important task that I know I could have easily completed. One of my goals is to be in excellent physical condition, which involves daily tasks of working out six times a week. To accomplish this goal, I have to possess the self-discipline to train six times per week, whether I feel like it or not.

I believe all of us have a little Tonto Kowalski inside, and he will come out on occasion to keep us on track. But here's the deal: if I had not set getting in excellent physical condition as a goal and my daily task list did not have working out on it, then Tonto would not have come out!

Bottom line—it is very hard to practice self-discipline if you don't have goals and a game plan to achieve them. The more detailed your goals and game plans are, the easier it is to have self-discipline.

Every day in life, we must make many choices!

Self-discipline is the ability to make the choice that does not always offer immediate satisfaction but will yield the greatest long-term reward.

Many times, the choice that gives us immediate satisfaction ends up also giving us guilt, anxiety, and even stress, sometimes hours after we have made the decision. Sometimes it's the next day or weeks later. Haven't you done this with food? You eat something because you had the craving and it was available, and hours later you say to yourself (or Tonto says to you), "What the hell did you eat that for?" My clients do this often. In between sets, they will pause for a few seconds, look down at the ground, and say to me, "I was bad yesterday." Like they are in the confessional at church, they share with me the bad food choices they made the day before. Now they feel guilty from making those choices.

Chapter 4 – Self-discipline

Simply put—self-discipline is making the correct decisions at all times, in all situations. Make choices that truly bring you closer to the important goals you have set for yourself!

Chapter 5 – What Drives Successful People?

> It's not how hard you hit, but how hard you can get hit and keep moving forward.
>
> —Rocky Balboa

I have been fortunate to train some very successful people in the past ten years, including professional athletes, Olympic athletes, CEOs, famous lawyers, TV celebrities, professional singers, movie producers, doctors, psychiatrists, police officers, and even Miss Teen Venezuela. I define successful people not by their money and material things. I admire the balanced, exciting lives they live along with the cool goals and accomplishments they have achieved.

I asked many of these people the same question: "You have achieved some remarkable things in your life and have reached a very high level of success in many areas. If you could give me just one word that describes how you got to this point in your life, what would that word be?"

I would like to share their responses with you. I am changing their names because information that is shared with a personal trainer is confidential. I am sure, though, that none of them would mind seeing their names in this book associated with great levels of success, and I imagine they would all be happy to contribute to my first book.

Chapter 5 – What Drives Successful People?

First, I will describe "Derek." I have a lot of fun taking him through workouts; he works very hard and is in tremendous shape. He is the CEO of a few companies, and he flies his own jet. He has two houses and two large boats—one in Canada and one in Florida. He even owns a castle in Germany.

When I asked him, "What one word describes how you became so successful?"

He looked at me and said, "That's a real good question." He thought about it for a moment, and then said, "Tenacity!" He told me that when he takes on a project or is in the boardroom, he is tenacious. He said no one could keep up with him. He'll get up earlier, work later, and do what it takes to win.

> *Tenacity*: persistent determination; to stick with something even when the going gets tough. Never give up. Never surrender!

The next person, "Gary," works in the insurance business. I imagine you are thinking, "What's the big deal about being an insurance guy?" Well, Gary handles multimillion-dollar insurance policies for professional athletes and large companies. He travels around the world for some of his clients, and some polices are in the billions. I never knew there was that much money in insurance. In addition to having this great career, he has a tremendous family life with a wife and three kids. He has also completed seven marathons, including one in Paris and one in London.

When Gary broke his right leg, he just adjusted his fitness goals and kept on training. We focused on a bigger, stronger chest and more defined abs. (Side note: he did not break his leg training with me; he did it while traveling.)

When I asked him for a one-word description, he said, "Perseverance!" He explained that when he commits to something worthwhile, he continues to pursue that goal no matter what obstacles might interfere.

> *Perseverance*: continued effort to do or achieve something despite difficulties, failure, or opposition.

"Alexandra" works with CEOs and CFOs for a huge health care company. You might say she keeps them all in line and handles many cost-saving projects that keep the company profitable. When an important presentation needs to be put together, she is the one who assembles it, gives it to the big dogs, and explains to them how to deliver it.

When I asked her for a word, she said, "Confidence!" She said, "I am not afraid to speak my mind when I know I am right. A lot of people," she said, "will not do that."

> *Confidence*: sure of oneself; having no uncertainty about one's own abilities, correctness, and successfulness; bold, trustful, or confiding.

"Jake" has achieved some remarkable things. He is a published author, a singer with many CDs and videos, and a film director/producer. And he even told me that one year, he was the highest-paid male suit model in the world. I could go on and on about what this man has accomplished.

Chapter 5 – What Drives Successful People?

When I asked him to give me one word to describe why he is successful, he replied, "I never give up." I reminded him that was more than one word. He then told me a few fascinating stories about how he never quit. He then said, "If I have to give just one word, it would be 'believe.' If you truly believe you can accomplish something, you will achieve that goal."

Jake told me that he wrote his first book when he was seventeen years old. Seventy-six publishers turned him down. The seventy-seventh time he sent his book to a publisher, a woman wrote him back and told him four or five things she did not like about the book. At first he was a little insulted; then he changed the things she did not like and sent it back to her. She again sent it back with more things she still did not like. This went on for a year and a half, and then one day, Jake got a letter from her in the mail. The only thing inside the envelope was her business card, and on the back it read, "Perfect." That book would later be made into a movie.

> *Believe*: to accept as true or real; to credit with veracity; to expect or suppose; to have firm faith, especially religious faith; to have faith, or trust; to have confidence in the truth or value of something.

Do you think it is a coincidence that the word *confidence* is in the definition of "believe"?

I believe we need to dig a little deeper. What really drives these people to be the best? I think it is a burning desire to never settle—an inner voice (perhaps Tonto's) that constantly tells them they can do better! They are in a competition with themselves to outdo their previous performances. The sky is the limit for these people; no achievement they desire is too big.

Are people born with this inner power? Is it something people can learn? Is it developed over time? Can a past event motivate people's present and future?

I believe the answer is yes to all of those questions. Bottom line—you can get your motivation from many places.

Motivation is a by-product of taking action and working hard on the daily tasks targeted at achieving your goals. When you set goals, plan your day around those goals, and work hard at it, you get motivated!

Taking action is the key! All the best plans, thoughts, and ideas are really worthless unless you physically go to work on the tasks that will help you reach your goal. Sometimes, following through is not easy, and that is what really separates the most successful people from those who enjoy the couch too much!

Right now, it is Sunday afternoon. There is a great football game on TV: the Denver Broncos versus the Philadelphia Eagles. And this little temptation guy keeps popping up on my shoulder, saying, "Take a break. Go into the living room and watch some football on your forty-inch HDTV. Grab an ice-cold Bud Light out of the fridge and kick back. You deserve it; you worked hard all week!"

Now, Tonto pops up on my other shoulder. He is on an action-motivator roll. He says, "No, Tom, you have in your daily plan to write, research, and work on your book for three hours. Not until you get that done can you watch football!" If I had not written down my goals and daily action plan this morning, Tonto might lose the fight. But he's been working out and getting stronger. He very rarely loses nowadays. He knocks that temptation guy out cold, and I complete my three-hour task. You gotta love that Tonto Kowalski!

Chapter 6 – Exercise

When I got my first set of weights in the sixth grade, it came with a fold-out poster showing fifteen different exercises you could do with the set. It was a 115-pound set of cement-filled plastic weights with a barbell and dumbbells. Till this day, it's the best present I can ever remember opening. I didn't know any better at the time; I just thought I was supposed to do one set of each exercise on the chart, twelve to fifteen reps every day.

There are people today that would absolutely benefit from doing that exact program. Are there better programs to meet certain needs? Absolutely! Doing something always beats doing nothing!

What is the best program for you? It depends on your fitness goals, any injuries you might have, your nutrition habits, and your motivation level.

Let's look at two types of programs: resistance training and cardiovascular training.

Resistance training can be your use of free weights, machines, body-weight exercises, resistance bands, TRX, kettlebells, and cable machines (basically, it is lifting or moving any type of weight).

Cardiovascular training can include walking, jogging, running, playing any sport, speed and agility drills, and plyometrics (any movement that elevates your heart rate).

Thousands of different combinations of activities from these two groups can form a great workout. The trick is to find combinations that you enjoy doing, make you feel good, and are designed to help you achieve your fitness goal!

My general rule: working out two or three times a week is for general maintenance, such as sustaining your current health and possible disease prevention. Working out five or six times a week with the right program can change your body and your life.

Next, how long do you work out? The answer depends on your goals.

Years ago, I believed that I needed at least an hour to work out. If I couldn't get to the gym for at least an hour, I wouldn't go. Then I decided that if I could get in a productive, thirty-minute workout, that would be much better than not working out at all.

Yesterday, I did a terrific nineteen-minute workout. I actually designed it for one of my extremely busy clients, and I put a lot of thought and science into it. It is planned to be a thirty-minute workout for the average person. I would like to share this thirty-minute workout with you. Let's give it a name: "Tonto on the Warpath."

Tonto on the Warpath

Warm up with:

    Twenty jumping jacks, fifteen body-weight squats, and ten push-ups

    Take a few deep breaths and go again with a few more reps.

Chapter 6 – Exercise

Twenty-five jumping jacks, twenty body-weight squats, and fifteen push-ups

Then rest for one minute.

Do the following four exercises in order, with no rest in between. Take one- to two-minute rests after completing all four. Repeat four times for a total of sixteen sets.

1. Alternating dumbbell chest press on a stability ball—twenty reps, ten each arm.

2. Row with resistance band in seated position—fifteen reps.

3. Dumbbell squat shoulder press—twelve reps.

4. Alternating high row with resistance band in a lunge position—twenty reps total, ten each arm. Switch legs at halfway point.

To cool down, do stretches. A TRX low-back stretch and TRX chest stretch are ideal. Do two sets of thirty seconds each. If TRX is not available, any effective traditional upper-body and lower-body stretch substitutions can be made.

The science behind the workout:

The warm-up is quick and efficient. It elevates the heart rate without using equipment, and the entire body gets warmed up. The repetitions can be adjusted to match your current fitness level.

The exercises are set up in a push, pull, push, pull sequence so that certain muscles can relax or become stabilizers while the others are the predominate movers. The rep range between the exercises adds variation, resulting in improved overall conditioning. For example, the dumbbell squat press is a lower-rep range; use this exercise to challenge your strength. Go heavy, even if you end up with only six or eight reps. The exercises with twenty reps are designed to improve muscular endurance.

Here, I describe which muscles are targeted in the exercises and offer key points on form.

Exercise 1—Stability Ball/Dumbbell Alt Chest Press

Primary mover: Pectoralis major and minor

Secondary mover: Triceps and anterior deltoid

Stabilizers (working isometrically): Hamstrings, gluteus maximus, and all core muscles.

The knee joint should be at a right angle, and the hips should be up high enough so that the knee, hip, and shoulder form a straight line. When one arm comes down during the chest press, a right angle should form at the elbow. By doing this exercise one arm at a time, moving the weight away from the center line of your body activates your internal and external obliques.

Exercise 2—Band Row in Squat Position

Primary mover: Back muscles (latissimus dorsi, rhomboids, and middle and lower trapezius)

Secondary mover: Rear deltoids, erector spinae, and serratus posterior

Stabilizers (working isometrically): Quadriceps, gluteus maximus, and all core muscles.

Staying in that seated position really works the quadriceps. A right angle should form at the hip and knees. Shoulders should be retracted

and located directly above the hips. Knees should be directly above the ankles. Back should be straight.

Exercise 3—Dumbbell Squat with Shoulder Press

Primary mover: Quadriceps, gluteus maximus, and deltoids

Secondary mover: Triceps and hamstrings

Stabilizers: Core muscles for controlling your balance.

Drive through your heels; don't let your heels come off the ground. Keep your knees behind your toes without flexing your back. Keep your back straight. This is a great total-body exercise, a power movement; it should be explosive so that you are firing all muscles in sequence.

Exercise 4—Alternating Band High Row in Lunge Position

Primary mover: Rear deltoids, upper and middle trapezius, latissimus dorsi, and rhomboids

Secondary mover: Teres major and minor, lower trapezius, serratus posterior, and internal and external obliques

Stabilizers: Core muscles for controlling your balance and keeping your back straight.

All your leg muscles are working isometrically as you hold in the lunge position. When you alternate the reps one hand at a time until you form a nice right angle at the elbow joint, it fires up the oblique muscles and strengthens the core.

These are four of my favorite and most effective exercises that provide a lot of bang for the buck. Try them out with good, proper form, and I believe you will like the results.

Please don't feel you have to get all scientific about your workout program. Always remember that something is better than nothing! Start with something, learn to like it, and then increase the challenge appropriately so that you are continually improving!

Last week, I went out for a run with one of my clients. There is a beautiful two-and-a-half-mile walking/jogging trail close to the gym. It surrounds an industrial park with many businesses in it. Over two thousand people work in that industrial park, and we occasionally see some of them actually walking or jogging during their break times, which I think is great.

So, on this day we decided to make a bet. I bet my client a coffee that we would see more people out smoking cigarettes than we would see walking or jogging.

I won the bet—we saw eleven people out smoking and *zero* people out exercising!

This just says something about our society. I don't understand it. I watched cigarette smoking put my mom's life through hell, and I have watched exercise improve so many lives.

To me, it's obvious. Next time you feel like having a cigarette, go for a walk instead!

I was driving home from Starbucks, a place I love to go and write while enjoying a triple espresso. It was Friday night, around 10:00 p.m., and I had written my target number of pages for the day. I decided to reward myself with a cold beer at Sylvan Street Grill. As I walked in, a man asked me for an ID. I told him it was out in the car. He said, "You need to go get it." I said OK and went out to my car.

On my way out and back, I felt a smile spreading across my face. I went up to the young man and said with a grin, "Here you go, my friend."

Chapter 6 – Exercise

He looked surprised when I called him a friend; after all, he had just insisted that I go out into the cold for my ID. Then he looked at it and exclaimed, "Wow!"

I said, "Yeah, I am turning fifty in three months."

He said, "Wow! A young fifty!"

Now, I bring up this exchange for one reason. A lot of people are very surprised when I tell them my age. If anyone asked me, "What would you say is the number one reason you look much younger than your age?" I would answer, "I work out daily!" I have worked out religiously since I got that weight-lifting set in sixth grade. I am not sure *religiously* is the correct word, actually; I don't want God getting mad at me. But the truth is, over the past thirty-eight years, it's been a very rare occurrence for me to go three days in a row without working out.

One of my current clients is approaching sixty, but he looks like he is in his forties. He said to me, "Last year I worked every day but three." He exercised 362 days out of 365! That's a fantastic accomplishment, and it pays back tremendous rewards. He is incredibly successful, and I attribute some of that success to his commitment to regular exercise.

I work part time as a bartender, as I mentioned earlier. One customer comes in often and calls me "Jack LaLanne." Now, some people might get offended being called the wrong name again and again. When he yells over the crowd, "Hey, Jack LaLanne, get me another Captain and Coke!" I just smile and say, "Coming right up!"

To me, that's an incredible compliment! Jack LaLanne was a pioneer in the fitness industry. His accomplishments are ridiculously incredible! His TV show was the longest-running fitness program in history—thirty-four years. He has been called "the godfather of fitness." In 1936, at the age of twenty-one, he opened the very first modern health club.

He designed and developed fitness equipment based on principles that are still used today.

Jack LaLanne lived till he was ninety-six, which is proof that exercise and working out will help you live longer. A good friend of mine went to Jack's ninety-fifth birthday party. He worked for Jack at one time and could not say enough good things about him. He said that Jack went around the room that day, and when he met someone a little out of shape, he poked the person in the belly and asked, "When are you going to do something about that?" I love that guy; I wish I had had the chance to meet him. If anyone else wants to call me Jack LaLanne, feel free.

Bottom line—exercise makes you feel better, can increase your lifespan, makes you more productive at work, makes you smarter, and allows you to do all the things you want to do for a long time.

So include working out in your daily routine. It will improve every aspect of your life!

> Physical fitness is not only one of the most important keys to a healthy body; it is the basis of dynamic and creative intellectual activity.
>
> —John F. Kennedy

Chapter 7 – Nutrition

Eating is one of life's great treasures. I love to eat! Some people perceive eating as just fueling the body, but others really enjoy the art of dining. Me and Tonto love both! He will tell me when to relax and enjoy a nice meal and when to just fuel. Nutrition is also one of my favorite topics to discuss, and apparently, I am not alone. Few other topics are covered in so many books and articles. I do feel bad for some people out there trying to understand nutrition, what they should be eating, how much they should they be eating, and when should they be eating. There is an overwhelming amount of information out there, and it keeps changing. One day, the yolk in the egg is bad for you; the next day, it contains all sorts of great nutrients for your body. One day, whole-grain products are great for you; the next day, they are not. For this reason, I am going to keep nutrition as simple as one-two-three:

1. Food shopping

2. Planning and food preparation

3. Self-discipline

I have taken many courses and have done a lot of studying on the topic of nutrition; however, I have probably learned as much or more from working with my clients.

I have performed over seven thousand one-on-one personal training sessions. Over the course of my fitness career, some clients have lost weight, some struggled to lose weight, and some have added muscle mass. I have noted the progress of my clients while discussing and following their eating habits and exercise programs, so I have a great deal of real-life data on the topic of nutrition and performance.

I can tell forty minutes into a workout whether or not the client had a nutritious meal an hour and a half before. I have seen clients crash just thirty-five minutes into their workouts because they didn't eat correctly and their bodies didn't have enough fuel.

The other interesting fact that I have learned is that three out of four clients know what they should be eating; they just don't have the self-discipline to make the right choices. Many know their nutritional flaws. They will say to me, "My problem is ice cream late at night," or "I skip breakfast," or "I go from noon till eight at night without eating anything, and then I am starving, and I have a huge meal—usually with pasta and wine." I ask a lot of my clients to give me a three-day food journal containing what they ate, when they had it, and the amount of each item. I was reviewing one of my client's journals and came across an entry for "thirty-seven Oreo cookies at 10:00 p.m." Tonto would have stopped this person at three cookies (or prevented them from having any).

Now, for some of you, as you read the paragraph above, something jumped out at you and you said, "I know where my flaw is, and I know what I need to change." Correct?

Before we get back to as simple as one-two-three, let us take a quick look at our macronutrients: protein, carbohydrates, and fats.

Protein: Our bodies use protein to build and repair tissue and cells. Proteins are broken down into amino acids, which are critical building blocks that promote strong bones, muscle, organs, cartilage, blood, and skin.

Chapter 7 — Nutrition

Carbohydrates: Our bodies use carbohydrates as a main source of fuel. Carbs break down into glucose, which our brain primarily runs on. Carbs are stored in our tissues and muscles in the form of glycogen, which we use as an energy source. Carbs are needed for the central nervous system, the kidneys, and the heart to function properly.

Fat: Our bodies use fat for transporting and absorbing vitamins A, D, E, and K. Fat is the most concentrated source of energy. Fat maintains cell membranes and promotes healthy skin. Fat provides cushioning and protection for the organs.

So, let's make sure we have a sufficient amount of these three macronutrients in our plan. To fool around and experiment with reducing and eliminating any of these macronutrients could result in a lack of fuel to support our systems in the body. All are important and have their role!

There is an example shopping list in the back of the book, Appendix A. If we measure the percentage of these three macronutrients in this list, it will show as follows:

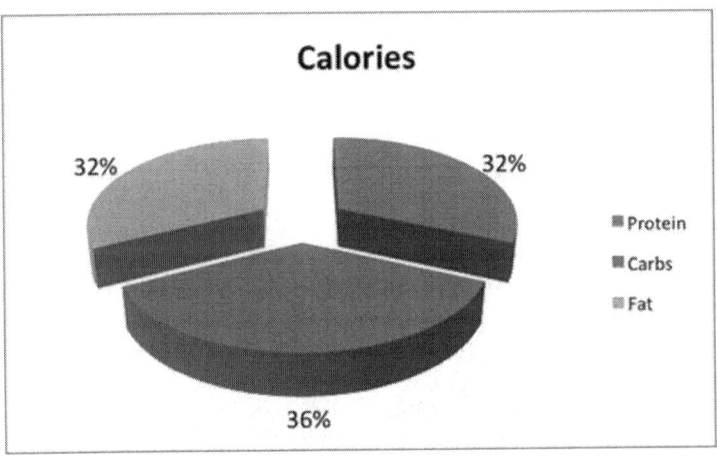

I believe this ratio contains sufficient amounts of macronutrients, proteins, carbs, and fats.

OK, back to simple as one-two-three:

1. Food Shopping

    You need to buy the right stuff (the sample shopping list in the back of the book is broken down by item in Appendix B).

    When food shopping, here are seven things to keep in mind:

    - You cannot go wrong with vegetables!

    - Fruits are terrific. Keep them in moderation, though, if you are watching your sugar intake.

    - Lean proteins like fish, chicken, turkey, lean beef, and eggs are great.

    - Nuts, like almonds and cashews, along with virgin olive oil, provide great fats.

    - Brown rice, sweet potatoes, and Ezekiel bread provide great fuel.

    - Reduce or avoid refined carbohydrates, sugary products, and processed foods.

    - Read labels. Look at serving size, calories, protein, fats, carbohydrates, sodium, sugar, and ingredients. Remember, the fewer ingredients, the better.

Chapter 7 — Nutrition

2. Planning and Food Preparation

You can plan to eat at a nice place where you can order a nutritious meal. You can also prepare meals ahead for the next day. The key is, have a plan! Here is where the question comes in: "How many times should I eat per day?" I will answer that with, "It depends on your fitness goal." For most people—85 percent—I say that three meals per day and two healthy snacks between meals is sufficient. An example:

> Breakfast: Two eggs, five ounces lean steak, one slice whole wheat bread, one banana, and ten ounces skim milk.
>
> Midmorning snack: One apple and twenty almonds
>
> Lunch: Six ounces chicken, one cup brown rice, one cup broccoli
>
> Midafternoon snack: Two chocolate rice cakes and twenty cashews
>
> Dinner: Eight ounces salmon and a large spinach salad
>
> Naturally, you can adjust this to your preferences. Just swap out proteins for proteins, carbs for carbs, and fats for fats.

3. Self-discipline

This is making yourself shop for the right stuff, plan your nutrition for the day, and sticking to it. That is the key!

This is where Tonto comes in and keeps you on track. If you buy the right stuff and plan your meals, Tonto will pop up on your shoulder and yell into your ear to do the right thing!

Many people will agree with me that eating and drinking are one of life's greatest pleasures. I recall sitting down with a new member at the gym as a potential new client. He said to me, "I know I need your help with my exercise program, but I am not changing my eating habits. I love to cook and eat, and it is my favorite thing to do on the planet! I am not changing that for anyone."

I just said, "OK, fine. I understand; I love food too. Let's get to work on that exercise program." In that same vein, I recently sat down to a meal consisting of two boiled lobsters, a one-and-a-half-pound porterhouse steak, two ears of corn on the cob, a Caesar salad, and two glasses of Sauvignon Blanc. Yes, it was my birthday. I was in heaven, and I ate everything. I love to eat.

When discussing nutrition, I feel two words are very important: *balance* and *moderation*.

When I say *balance*, I mean that I believe it is important to eat a wide variety of foods from all the important food groups so that the body gets all the proper nutrients to function effectively. These nutrients support and maintain the systems that keep us healthy. When I say *moderation*, I am talking portion size and frequency. Too much of any food can result in weight gain. I know a person who read a number of articles about the benefits of eating butter. My advice to this person was that throwing half a stick of butter into a meal probably wouldn't help, but a teaspoon might be fine. That's what I mean with moderation.

To improve your eating habits, identify the foods in each of the three groups that you *enjoy* eating. For example:

Chapter 7 – Nutrition

Protein—haddock, shrimp, chicken, beef, turkey, and eggs

Carbohydrates—pasta, bread, cereal, apples, bananas, grapes, carrots, string beans, and salad

Fats—almonds, cashews, sunflower seeds, and olive oil

Remember to focus on foods you take pleasure in. I don't think it makes any sense to develop a nutrition plan based on foods you don't like to eat; you won't follow the plan. Your list might look very different from the one listed above, and it can be much longer.

Here are some guidelines based on what I have seen with my clients and experimented with in my own nutrition plan:

I do believe that whole-grain products digest slower and provide a longer range of fuel for energy. Refined carbohydrates (white bread, crackers, cakes, cookies, and other sugary snacks) digest quicker, raise insulin levels, provide less fuel for energy, provide fewer nutrients, and could slow down metabolism.

Recently, there has been new research regarding whole wheat and whole grain products. What I have learned is that the same thing does not work for everyone, we all have different lifestyles and genetic makeups. I have one client that hit a plateau. She ended up getting tremendous results when she switched to a strict Paleo diet with no breads or grains. I tried it, but it did not work for me. I did not feel as sharp and did not have the same energy I had before. I really missed my two slices of 100% whole wheat bread or Ezekiel bread for breakfast. Again, moderation is the key, two slices in the morning works for me, six slices per day might not.

Lets talk pasta for a minute, a lot of people's favorite, including my own. I used to cook up a pound of white pasta and eat it in two meals. Today that would not work for me based on my fitness and health goals and wouldn't work for most people. It took me a while to switch over to 100% whole wheat pasta and I am fine with it now. The other big difference is the portion size I am now having. I will cook up a box of whole wheat pasta, which is usually 13.25 ounces and divide it into five 9oz containers. That's only 2.65oz per container, then add the lean protein and veggie and you have some great fuel.

Monounsaturated and polyunsaturated fats have been thought of as good fats, and saturated and trans as the bad ones. Recent research has also come up with new results stating that saturated fats are not linked to heart disease. I will not get into that debate, I will stick to moderation and say a teaspoon of butter might work for you and a stick a day might not. So just make your list of favorite healthy foods using common sense. Eat whole-grain products in moderation, eliminate or reduce refined carbohydrates and sugary products, limit saturated fat and eliminate or reduce trans fat intake. Tonto will say it too, moderation and balance is the key!

Veggies—who really craves and loves vegetables? When was the last time one of your friends called you up and said, "Oh my God, I'm dying for some spinach and broccoli! I know this great spinach-and-broccoli place over on First Avenue. Want to meet me there for a bite and a beverage?" Happens to you all the time, right? I imagine not. But now replace spinach and broccoli with Chinese food, pepperoni pizza, or cheeseburgers, and it sounds familiar.

Some people really do like vegetables. But many people only eat them because they know they are healthy. If potato chips or French

Chapter 7 – Nutrition

fries were just as nutritious as vegetables, there wouldn't be much of a contest between them.

On the news the other day, the announcers were talking about how eating healthy can be very expensive. But it is possible to eat healthy and stick to a budget. That shopping list in the back of the book, Appendix A, is for a 2,500-calorie-per-day meal plan for one person, and in this case it cost around fifty-seven dollars for the week.

I do consider food to be fuel for the body, just like gas for a car. The list in the back of the book, contains approximately 2500 calories per day, and that's what my body runs well on. If we break that down even further, it's around 105 calories per hour. My truck gets twenty miles per gallon, so if I put in three gallons of gas, I can drive for sixty miles. When the tank is almost empty, a yellow warning light comes on. We all have a similar kind of signal in our bodies that comes on when our tanks are empty. I could be talking with someone, and I'll say that my yellow warning light just came on and that I need to go put in some fuel. Of course, some people look at me a little strange, but most know exactly what I'm talking about. If I only need one hour's worth of fuel, 105 calories, to get me to my next meal, I might just eat a banana. If I need two hours' worth of fuel, I could eat twenty-five almonds.

How many calories does your body need to run efficiently? Here's a guideline:

Weight (lbs.)	_Calories per hour_	
100	75	(1,800/day)
125	85	(2,040/day)
150	95	(2,280/day)

175	105	(2,520/day)
200	115	(2,760/day)
225	125	(3,000/day)

Note: the weight number above is your ideal weight; it might not be your current weight. Also, this is just a guideline, a starting point, and probably needs to be adjusted based on your activity level and fitness goal.

Water—I will not take up your time listing all the benefits of water. Keeping it simple: without water, we die. How much water should we have per day? Many books and magazines state that we should drink sixty-four ounces per day, which is not a bad place to start. One serving of bottled water often contains five hundred milliliters. Drinking four bottles of water per day is equivalent to two liters, which is about sixty-four ounces. In most cases, that should be your minimum per day. Take into consideration your size, body composition, activity level, exercise program, and environment, and increase your intake accordingly.

OK, I have spent the last month researching and studying all the vitamins and minerals our bodies need. There is tons of information out there. I learned a lot, and I will continue to learn. So I have concluded that it is such an important topic that it will get its own book—my second book, coming soon!

I want to sum up what I have learned so far about vitamins and minerals, though, to give you some guidelines for your nutrition plan.

An example of a nutritious day of food is as follows:

- Two pieces of fruit per day (e.g., banana, apple)

Chapter 7 – Nutrition

- Three servings of vegetables per day (e.g., carrots, salad, broccoli)

- Three servings of a whole-grain product or starchy carbohydrate (e.g., whole wheat bread, brown rice, whole wheat pasta, sweet potato)—approximately fifty grams per serving

- Four servings of lean protein per day (e.g., eggs, turkey, chicken, fish)—approximately four to five ounces per serving

- Half a gallon of water per day

In most cases, the foods in this list cover your vitamins and minerals needed for the day. Strive to divide those foods equally between four or five meals, eating every three hours. Eating this way will likely speed up your metabolism and give you a sustained, high energy level throughout the day.

Very important: certain medical conditions won't allow a person to eat some of these foods. If you have such a condition, consult with your doctor and/or a registered dietician before changing what you eat.

Also, this daily guideline is targeted at a person weighing around 175 pounds. Portion size should be adjusted to match your size, activity level, and fitness goals.

So, remember, first make time in your busy schedule to buy the right stuff! If you don't have the right kinds of food available and you get hungry, you are going to eat whatever is there. That's our human instinct. Second, make time in your busy schedule to plan and prepare your meals for the next day. Yes, this takes self-discipline!

Clean out your cabinets. Get rid of those refined carbohydrates, processed foods, sugary snacks, and foods high in saturated and trans fat. Your local church or food pantry will gladly take those off your hands. You may want to set up one cabinet for your kids' snacks. Just stay out of that cabinet and start getting your kids hooked on healthier snacks like grapes and nuts.

Food for Thought

Be careful where you get your nutritional advice. One night while bartending, I was waiting on two people. I brought over two glasses of water for them with a lemon wedge in each glass.

One of them took the lemon wedge out and said, "No, no, no—too many carbs in that. I have been cutting carbs out of my diet, and it's working great." This person went on to talk about her eating plan, and I was amazed by how many other people started listening to the conversation. Based on this person's size and physique, I was surprised that other people would be so interested in what she ate.

Over the next three hours, these two people sat and ate and drank and ate and drank. That lemon wedge pulled out of the water glass for having too many carbs was probably the healthiest thing I served them the whole time!

> The doctor of the future will no longer treat the human frame with drugs, but rather will cure and prevent disease with nutrition.
>
> —Thomas Edison

Chapter 8 – Attitude Can Shift All Things in Your Favor

I can't emphasize enough the importance of a positive, high-energy attitude.

It is the one thing you have 100 percent control of. You can determine and choose what type of attitude you have every day!

We all have major difficulties in our lives that could easily upset us if we let them. Everyone has these difficulties, and most people let them affect their attitude.

You can set your attitude at the beginning of each day. Without question, when you start your day, someone will ask you, "How are you?" And that will happen many times during the day. So why not have an answer ready each day? I always do, and it will usually be one of the following words:

- Excellent

- Terrific

- Outstanding

- Fantastic

- Awesome

And no matter what type of problems, difficulties, and issues I might have at the time, I still use one of those words (except at wakes and funerals).

One of the most powerful things that I have learned is this: If you don't let the negative attitude or behavior of other people affect your own positive attitude, you will be incredibly successful.

This is not easy, and it takes practice. One reason it is not easy is that it happens all the time. You will encounter so many knuckleheads during the course of a day; it is very hard not to let them affect your attitude.

I often repeat a phase in my head that I call "Smile at the knuckleheads." I used to get so aggravated by people talking on their cell phone out in public and especially at the gym. The people who never put their weights away at the gym or are loud and obnoxious used to aggravate me. Now they don't bother me, and I don't let them affect my attitude or knock me off track. I just simply look at them, smile, and say in my head, "What a doofus. You're in the 3 percent group." You see, I learned years ago, from my friend Phil, who has been in the fitness industry for thirty years, that those people will always exist. He said, "You can count on 3 percent of your member base being knuckleheads. And if you ship those 3 percent to a deserted island, another 3 percent will grow out of the corners of the gym. Misguided people with improper values will always be out there. I believe that 3 percent exist in most businesses. It is important to never let oppositional people knock us off our path in life.

> "Napoleon Hill and W. Clement Stone both were
> under the opinion that ultimate personal success could
> be achieved by sporting a positive mental attitude."
>
> —Andrew Carnegie

Chapter 8 – Attitude Can Shift All Things In Your Favor

Let me give you some examples of the power your attitude has:

When I was working in Germany, I was the production manager for a shift of 273 people running eleven different production lines. I found that I could control the attitude and morale of the entire shift. I would walk up and down the production lines with a smile, greet people, and say, "Wie gehts?" Which basically means, "How's everything?" They would respond and then ask me the same question. I would reply, "Ausgezeichnet!" which means "Excellent!" or "Terrific!" I chose to greet everyone with an extremely positive and high-energy attitude and recognize all the people. At this facility, that was not a normal custom.

Mary Kay Ash said: "There are two things people crave more than sex and money, and that is praise and recognition."

Other peoples' attitude will always reflect your own attitude. If you are confrontational and negative toward people, chances are they will act the same way toward you. If you are positive and happy, they will be too.

I can recall my first personal training job at Gold's Gym in Salisbury, Massachusetts. This was a large gym, with over six thousand members. It was the third-largest Gold's Gym in the world at that time. I knew I would always have to have a very positive attitude in order to succeed. After working there for about one year, I walked by a group of guys who were there almost every day. They asked me how I was doing, and I replied "Excellent!" As I moved past them, I heard one of the guys say to the others, "Just once, only once, I want to hear that kid say he was lousy!" I looked back at him, smiled, and said, "Never going to happen; it's not allowed!"

A person's attitude can be interpreted over the phone, in e-mail, and even in text messages. Which words are used and how they are said can give you an idea about how someone really feels. I have left phone messages for new members at the gym to confirm their first appointment for a fitness evaluation. Some of them have said to me, "I could feel your energy through that voice mail you left me." That's a great feeling.

A few years ago an individual who worked for me got in an argument with our general manager. And then he did a few other things that resulted in his employment ending suddenly. Whether he quit or got fired is really irrelevant to this story.

I received an e-mail from this person the following week, and I could feel his anger, frustration, and bitterness toward the company through the words he had typed. He made some statements involving me, which I felt were inappropriate and not accurate.

I started writing an e-mail back to clarify some things and stick up for the company and myself. As I was writing, I could feel my anger and temper rising, and I knew this wasn't a positive letter. Then Tonto popped up on my shoulder and said, "Stop writing. Relax, Tom. Take a few deep breaths, delete this e-mail, and write one tomorrow."

The next day, I wrote the return e-mail, and I made sure it was positive. This individual was a good worker, did many good things for the company, and helped a lot of people. In the e-mail, I thanked this person for his efforts while he was employed at the company, and I wished him all the best as he traveled along his career path.

I did get a response, and I swear, it came from a different person. He thanked me for acknowledging his work and wishing him success. He wrote that he appreciated my efforts and wished me well.

CHAPTER 8 – ATTITUDE CAN SHIFT ALL THINGS IN YOUR FAVOR

The point of this story is to prove that people will always respond to you in a positive way, whether it's in person, via e-mail, or in a text, if you are respectful and affirmative in your interactions!

Another example of how maintaining a positive attitude can benefit you is when you encounter two people arguing or fighting over something. This can create an uncomfortable situation for many people.

Two guys can act childish when they start yelling at each other and calling each other names, even if one of them is around forty and the other is around fifty. This happened at one of the gyms where I was working. Unfortunately, I've encountered situations like these more than once.

This particular time I was not in uniform, and I was trying to get in a workout.

I could have approached the guys abruptly and shouted, "Hey, knock that off! We don't tolerate that type of shit at this gym!" in an angry voice. One of them might have said, "Mind your own business. This guy's being an asshole…" and so on. Then the argument would have continued and maybe escalated. On another occasion, the police had to be called, and they removed the individual from the facility, banning him for good.

So instead, I said: "Hey, guys, what's the situation here? How can I help?" with a smile on my face. I was laughing inside because it was kind of comical—two grown men arguing over a four-by-four-foot space. I said, "The gym has sixty-seven thousand square feet, and there are over a hundred other places each one of you can do those movements." I showed them better places to do the exercises, and we all ended up happy.

It really is amazing how many benefits come from having a positive attitude. Other people benefit enormously from your behavior; however, you benefit even more! I know people who come into an establishment with a negative attitude, and it keeps them down and unhappy all day long. So, no matter what's going on in your life, when you go into work or a gathering and someone asks you, "How are you doing?" Say: "Fantastic!" and that will ignite you and keep you going all day long.

When I was managing new personal trainers, I would tell them to leave any problems and negative issues they might have outside the front door. I said, "Don't bring them in here. Stuff them in a big duffle bag and leave it right outside the front door. Don't worry—no one will steal it. It will still be there when you leave, and you can pick up the bag on your way out. If you bring that bag in here, it will affect your business." I used a trick when I entered the gym: I pictured a light switch on the wall, and I reached over and flicked the switch on. That would turn on my high-energy, positive attitude. Later, I added a dimmer switch to really crank it up!

The attitude you carry with you will dictate the perception people have of you and how they will describe you to other people!

> The greatest discovery of all time is that a person can change his future by merely changing his attitude.
>
> —Oprah Winfrey

Chapter 9 – Money

There was a time in my thirties when I could not spend money fast enough. I was earning lots and had few bills. I was generous with my money and would pick up the tab on many occasions. I would spoil people at Christmas and on their birthdays. I would blow money foolishly at bars and nightclubs on weekends. Every two weeks, another large sum of money would drop into my bank account, and I would spend it again.

Boy, I miss those days…

Well, actually, I did not have anything tangible at the time. I did not own a house. I even leased my car. I paid rent at an apartment complex. So, was I really wealthy?

If I had known then what I know now, I would have spent about half what I did on fun and entertainment and invested the other half into my 401k or other worthwhile investment. (More on investing coming up!) Now things are different. I don't have extra money to pick up the tab, buy expensive gifts, or spend foolishly on the weekends.

I do own three houses…wait a minute, let me rephrase that. The *banks* own three houses, and my name is on the mortgages. I do own my truck; I paid it off last year. So am I wealthier now than I was back then?

Well, honestly, I believe I would be in a better financial situation if I only had one or two houses. And I know I will get to that point within the next five years.

Now, I created my financial situation of not having extra money to spend as I please. After I had purchased my three houses, I decided to make a career change, as I mentioned earlier. I went from earning $453 per day to $20 a week. Yes, that's correct; I was in manufacturing/engineering, working as the plant operations manager for Gorton's of Gloucester, and I changed to the fitness industry and began working as a personal trainer. My first week in my new career, I trained one person and received twenty dollars for that week. At this gym, you only got paid when you trained someone. The following week, I trained three people. I have continued to grow my business to the point where I make good money.

I have no regrets with my career change, and I would do the same thing again. What I wish I could change is my previous spending habits. One of the smartest things I have learned and read is this: "It is not the amount of money you earn that makes you rich; it's the amount of money you spend that makes you rich." This was said by Paul Clitheroe, a financial analyst and financial advisor.

I did some simple math when I made my career change. I said to myself, "If you can make $50,000 per year doing personal training, $25,000 per year bartending, and $25,000 per year from rental income, that's $100,000 per year." A person can live very comfortably on $100,000 per year, especially being single with no kids and no student loans. The problem was that when I added up my yearly spending at that time, it was $137,000. That's when Tonto popped up on my shoulder and said, "What the hell are you doing? What are you spending all that money on?"

Tonto told me that I did not do two things that I should have done, and hopefully you can learn from my mistakes. I did not change my spending habits when I made the career change, and I did not add up all the utilities and maintenance costs of owning three houses. Once I realized it, I started tracking every dollar I spent each day. I plugged

Chapter 9 – Money

all expenses into an Excel spreadsheet and started to learn where my money was going and how I could make improvements to yield a positive cash flow for the year.

Now I have a monthly budget set up, and I track every dollar I spend. I encourage you to do the same if money is an issue for you at this time. The budget covers my mortgages, utilities, estimated maintenance costs, loans, food, clothes, social life, and so on, in over thirty categories. Every time I spend money, I ask for a receipt or record it on a small piece of paper and put that paper in a pile on my desk at home. Once or twice a week, I enter my expenditures into the Excel spreadsheet with my monthly budget. An Excel spreadsheet works great for me; however, I would do this with a spiral notebook and a calculator if I didn't use the computer.

The cool part is that at the end of the month, I compare my budget spending to my actual spending. Then I take my total actual spending and compare that number to the amount of money I earned for the month, which is my take-home pay. On an Excel spreadsheet, this is cool, because you get to make that box turn red if it's negative or black if it's positive. That's why I love that AC/DC song, "Back in Black." You just need to stay in the black!

By planning and putting together a monthly budget, it gives Tonto the ammunition to help you when temptation comes your way. There is an example of monthly spending tracking in the back of the book (Appendix C). In this example, I ended up in the red. And I know exactly why. I had rental business expenses and maintenance costs that I did not budget for, and I spent more than I planned in a few other categories.

Many people out there will say, "Don't spend time tracking all those expenses; use the time to focus on increasing your earnings so you are always in the black." I do know some successful people who do exactly that, and it works for them. The quickest way to wealth, though, is do both at the same time. Cut back on your spending and increase the amount of money you earn.

Ben Franklin first said this back in 1758:

> *There are two ways of being happy: We may either diminish our wants or augment our means—either will do—the result in the same; and it is for each man or woman to decide for himself or herself, and do that which happens to be the easiest. If you are idle or sick or poor, however hard it may be to diminish your wants, it will be harder to augment your means. If you are active and prosperous or young and in good health, it may be easier for you to augment your means than to diminish your wants. But if you are wise, you will do both at the same time, young or old, rich or poor, sick or well; and if you are very wise you will do both in such a way as to augment the general happiness of society.*
>
> (Source: http://www.goodreads.com/quotes/150284-there-are-two-ways-of-being-happy-we-may-either)

Now, how much money do you want? An even better way to ask that question is: how much money do you need to live the way you want to live?

There have been many discussions about money versus happiness and which one is more important. The truth is, they are both very important. We need money to survive; it pays for food, a place to live, education, transportation, and all those types of things that are essential for our survival. And let's just face it: if we're not happy, what good

Chapter 9 – Money

is surviving? Money also buys things that make us happy. The key is balance! I found a chart that I think is pretty cool on correlating happiness and money:

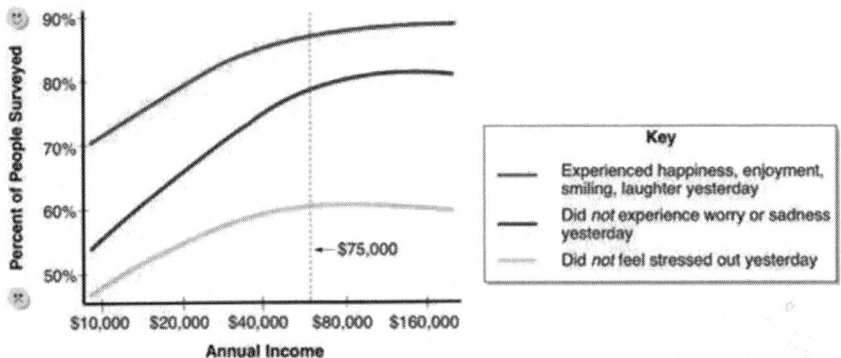

(Source: http://icanhasscience.com/psychology-stuff/actually-money-does-buy-happiness/)

Studies say that happiness levels out at $75,000 per year, and I agree. I believe this is an average, though; some people are happy earning much less, and some people are happy earning much more. Dealing with hundreds of clients, I have learned that, in most cases, people with higher-paying jobs (over $75,000) have higher stress levels, and that can affect happiness.

The people I know who earn well above $75,000 and are always happy, however, are the ones who truly enjoy what they are doing.

> Work at what you love to do, and you never have to work a day in your life!
>
> —Confucius

About ten years ago, I asked my dad a question related to this topic. This was well before he was diagnosed with dementia. I said to him, "Dad, you have held a lot of really good jobs in your career: director of food service at Rutgers University, director of food service at Boston University, director of food service at Lowell University, and president/owner of Catering by Bill Muser. Which was the best job you ever had?"

He looked at me and said, "That's a great question. Let me think about that." He took his time thinking. When he finally looked at me, to my surprise, he said, "I think it's the one I have right now." At that time, he was retired and working part time as a baker at a Stop and Shop supermarket.

You see, the other jobs were very stressful, and he worked long hours. In his current job at the time, no one reported to him, and he worked the hours he really enjoyed. He always loved to get up early in the morning. At the supermarket, he went to work at 4:00 a.m. and was done by 11:00 a.m. He worked seven hours, four days per week. He baked bread, made cookies, and decorated cakes. And he really enjoyed it.

Now, he had to work those other high-paying jobs before he retired. Being married and having six kids is not cheap. Mom had her hands full taking care of us brats. She didn't work outside the home; neither did my dad want her to find a paying job.

Sometimes you need to perform a job you are not crazy about for a while till you can get to a better place. There are also certain times in your life when you want to earn the most possible money and build your résumé. When I graduated from college, I actually got three job offers at the same time. My classmate and I were kind of in competition to see who could score the highest-paying job. So I chose to accept the salary with the highest dollar amount; I was an industrial engineer for the United Parcel Service (UPS) in New York

Chapter 9 – Money

City. I started off driving a big package truck to learn that part of the operation. I worked long hours, and it was not easy, but I did feel really cool driving a big truck through Manhattan. Eventually I realized that I had not calculated the cost of living when working in New York City. Apartments were too expensive in the city, so I chose to live in New Jersey. The commute to work was awful—bumper to bumper. And including the tolls, gas, and parking fees, it was ridiculous. When I added up all my expenses, including my student loans, I knew I couldn't sustain the job, even with my high salary. I lasted four months.

Today, I can really relate to my dad's situation. I managed people for over twenty-five years. I had to hire, train, write performance reviews, and deliver many disciplinary actions, including terminations. Today, working as a master trainer only, no one reports to me, and I have no conference calls and no meetings. I can make my own schedule, and I experience a lot less stress. Also, when I calculate how much I am earning against the hours I am working, I am earning more per hour than I was when I was a manager. I am sharing my story with you to encourage you to look at your career path from all angles. Take your time analyzing the pros and the cons of your decision.

I do plan on becoming a millionaire. I think it's a worthwhile goal, and it will allow me to live the rest of my life the way I want to live it. The latest statistics show that there are almost ten million millionaires in the United States today, so it is certainly achievable! Many people set becoming a billionaire as their goal. There are almost five hundred billionaires in the United States. If becoming a millionaire or multimillionaire excites you, why not set it as a goal? To be honest with you, being a multimillionaire or billionaire does not excite me. I don't need that much money to live the way I want to live.

To reach financial goals, don't spend money you don't have, and learn to enjoy saving and watching your investments grow.

Before you spend money, whether the item costs $25 or $2,500, ask yourself a few questions:

- Do I really need this?

- Is this purchase related to my goals?

- What happens if I don't buy this?

- Is this item a necessity or a luxury?

- Do I have something at home, in the attic, in the garage, or in the basement that I could use instead?

- What if I don't buy this and I invest this money in a savings plan?

- What if I put this money toward the principal on my mortgage or toward the down payment for my first house?

Now, please don't get me wrong. I am not saying you shouldn't have any fun in life. I am saying that if you are buried in debt, take some of these measures for a while, get yourself out of debt, and then start living like you want to live.

If you keep getting better at your job, your income will increase. But a lot of people increase their spending when their earnings increase. The trick is to increase your saving and investing when your income increases. Sure, you can reward yourself with something when you get that promotion; just don't get carried away.

Money is not everything! If you think about and talk about money all the time, most people won't want to hang around you, including your family. The people who will want to hang around are the ones who also allow money to consume their lives. Other people may want to use you for your money; they will expect you to pick up the tab each time you go out together and to buy them things. And if you are cool with that, then great.

I believe it is important to not let money consume your life. I want to hang with people and family that like me for being me, not because I have money and buy them things.

You need only so much money to live the way you want to live, and striving for that amount while not bragging about it is the way to go. I have missed some family events over the past few years because I didn't have the money to make the trip and/or take time off from work. That, to me, is unacceptable; I need to earn enough money so that I can be present when my family would like me to be.

The key is to strive for the amount you wish to earn that will allow you to live the way you want to live, without letting it affect the relationships you have with the people who mean the most to you!

I would like to close this chapter with something my dad said on the day of my mom's funeral. He said, "She never ever complained about not having enough money. If we had it, great—she would use it wisely. If it wasn't there, she would improvise. She never, ever, ever complained about not having enough money." He repeated this several times.

My brother and I looked at each other, just nodded our heads, and said, "So true!"

Chapter 10 – Investing and Saving

A two-hundred-dollar calf? I recently heard a true story that was amazing. A friend and coworker of mine from Brazil came to the United States when he was fifteen years old. He started working in restaurants as a busboy, as a waiter, and then as a bartender.

When he had saved up his first two hundred dollars at the age of fifteen, he sent it to his parents in Brazil to purchase a baby cow. His parents owned a farm, and they would raise the cow. In two years, the cow could be sold for fifteen hundred dollars. That was a great investment.

Over the next ten years, my friend bought many cows and sold them all at a profit. He bought land with the money he earned. He continued to invest in both cows and land. He worked many hours at the restaurant and did not waste money. He spent money on necessities only.

At the young age of twenty-five, he sold half of the land he had purchased. He received $770,000 for this land. He is now moving back to Brazil with his wife and son to live comfortably with the assets and money he has saved.

Hard work can definitely pay off! And, might I add, he provided exceptional customer service in the restaurant, which also yielded nice returns.

Another true, exceptional story: A pizza chef at the restaurant where I work was there for twelve years. He worked seven days a week

Chapter 10 – Investing And Saving

and twelve to fourteen hours per day. He rarely went out and lived very frugally. He sent his money back to his family and friends in Brazil.

Initially, he sent back enough money for his friends to purchase a truck, which they used to transport corn syrup. They would earn fifty dollars per trip. Over the course of twelve years, this business grew to the point where he had ten trucks and dozens of employees. His business is now worth around one million dollars, which is a lot of money in Brazil. He moved back to Brazil and is living very comfortably.

I am not saying you should work seven days a week or fourteen-hour days—not at all. I am against that. Five days a week and a maximum of ten hours per day is sufficient, provided you work efficiently and don't waste time.

What these two stories above illustrate is that a portion of your earnings, even at a young age, should go toward a worthwhile investment. The bigger that portion is, the greater the return.

Like I mentioned earlier, spend less than you earn, and invest the rest. If you earn a lot more than you spend, then you can invest more and have a greater return on investment.

Now, what do you invest in?

Real estate? A 401k or IRA savings plan? The stock market? Your own business?

I do not claim to be an expert on investments; if I were, I would be living in financial freedom right now. My expertise is in fitness and nutrition. However, I have learned some valuable things about investing and saving that I feel could benefit others. I definitely recommend that you do your homework on any investment. Study and research all the pros and the cons of the investment. Make sure you do the math on all of its costs and the projected income it will produce. Analyze the side effects it can have on your family and friends.

Let's start with real estate. My first investment was a $75,000 lot of land in the middle of a PGA golf course in Fort Myers, Florida. This was a half-acre lot. A few professional athletes also purchased lots in that development. This investment opportunity came from a good friend who was a millionaire and made a lot of money in the real estate market. He too bought a lot of land at this PGA golf course. Our plan was to sell our land in five to ten years and double our money. Sounds pretty good, doesn't it?

Five years later, I had a job opportunity to move to Germany for a couple of years. I wasn't sure what to expect, and I wanted to unload my real estate expense. It was costing me $535 per month. I had the property for five years, and I sold it for $75,000, the same amount I had purchased it for. Not a good investment. My friend held on to his for a few more years but did not do any better.

I could have invested $535 per month in a good IRA savings plan for that five years and then stopped. At an average interest rate of 8 percent, that money would be worth $145,154 right now, and $497,290 when I reach sixty-five, retirement age.

Half a million dollars! Are you kidding me? Is that all you have to do for half a million dollars? I was twenty-eight years old when I made that investment, and I sold it at age thirty-three.

Now, sure, I took a risk. It could have paid off big. We do need to take chances.

The lesson is, if you are around twenty-five to thirty years old, consider investing five hundred dollars a month. You can be pretty sure that if you invest that amount for just five years and then stop and

Chapter 10 – Investing And Saving

leave the money alone to earn interest, it could bring you an extra five hundred thousand dollars for your retirement. Like I mentioned earlier, if I knew then what I know now, I would have invested much more money from age twenty-five to thirty-five into my 401k or an IRA!

Now, let's talk houses. Currently, I have three houses. I do not have any kids of my own; I currently have seven awesome nieces and nephews, two of which are my goddaughters. But I do pay the mortgages on three houses, which I sometimes refer to as my kids! Conant the barbarian, Saint Joseph, and Sweet Isalene are my three kids.

Conant, which is actually located on Conant Street in Danvers, Massachusetts, was the first house I bought. Like the typical first child, this kid got everything: new rugs, new hardwood and tile floors, and a new bathroom.

Joseph, the middle kid, is a quiet, low-maintenance house. This house is actually located on Saint Joseph Street, Hyannis, Massachusetts. When I bought it, I did put on a new back deck, which cost around seven thousand dollars. I also added new tile floors; it helps to have a tile man in the family. My brother Marty is silly with the stuff, and he'll tile anything.

Then there is Sweet Isalene, actually located on Isalene Street, West Hyannisport, Massachusetts. Yes, this one is the girl, and the last child. And yes, she is spoiled and draining me of money. One expense was a brand-new $24,000 bathroom.

I must admit, this one gives me the most enjoyment; this is the beach house getaway. This is where I go and relax and forget about work. I am trying to figure out, though—if I go down there to relax, why do I end up doing all sorts of work on the house, trying to improve it? I am slowly but surely figuring out how to make Isalene maintenance free and do more relaxing than working when I am there.

The latest studies and research show that the average cost to raise a child, from birth till the eighteenth birthday, is $235,000. The average price I paid for each of my three houses is $240,667. That's pretty close.

Now I know that nothing can compare to all that's involved with raising a child and the joys and frustrations that you encounter along the way. From a financial point of view, though, I bet they are similar. When the market is up, of course, you can't go sell your kids, even though you might want to. There were probably times when my mom would have taken ten bucks to get rid of me. Do kids go up and down in value as time goes on? I don't think so. But houses can't talk back to you or swear at you.

Do unexpected expenses come up with both houses and kids? Absolutely! Do costs for maintaining your house and utility costs go up, like the costs for food, clothing, and education for your kids? Absolutely! That is really what I'm talking about. From a financial standpoint, raising a child can be compared to owning a home.

Right now, today, I am feeling really good about my Isalene house investment. And I just realized why: people are renting the house for the week at the price of $1,700. So now I can relax at my house in Danvers, enjoy this cup of coffee, and I have been paid for the week.

Some people say that real wealth is money coming in whether you are working or not. You can relax at your house, and checks just arrive in the mail or money gets automatically deposited into your bank account. Sounds pretty good, doesn't it? Heck, yeah!

Now, when my Cape Cod beach house is not rented and I am not there enjoying it, I get an uneasy feeling, like something is wrong.

Chapter 10 – Investing And Saving

Asset utilization percentage is a topic always discussed at manufacturing companies. Let us take a look at what we can learn from comparing production companies and the real estate market.

My first few years at Philips Lighting Company, I was put in charge of two production lines: unit twenty-four and unit twenty-five. When the lines were running, they each made forty fluorescent light bulbs per minute. That's twenty-four hundred bulbs per hour. There were thirty bulbs in a case, so that's eighty cases per hour. It was an eighty-hour shift, and it ran nonstop. A relief crew would take people's places for breaks and lunches. So, if there wasn't any downtime, each line would produce 640 cases for the shift at 100 percent efficiency.

Obviously, there was some downtime, though. Many pieces of equipment on the line could break down, and human error could cause a stop in production. So at the end of the shift, I had to calculate and report where every minute was lost. Each day, I reported efficiency for each production line. If the line only produced 576 cases for the shift, it ran at 90 percent efficiency, and forty-eight minutes would have to be accounted for. Usually, over 90 percent was good, and less than 90 percent was not good.

When the production line went down, the company would be losing eight hundred dollars per hour. So, if the line was down for any length of time, upper management would stop by, wondering what was going on. Not a fun visit!

I was extremely lucky my first few months there. Those production lines ran great, and I produced very good numbers. I got many pats on the back from upper management. I wasn't doing much, just hanging out on the production lines, encouraging and motivating workers (or, you might say, just shooting the shit with them…).

It's funny in the production/manufacturing world: when you work the hardest, dealing with all types of equipment and people problems that are out of your control, you end up producing bad numbers and getting yelled at. When you work the least and everything is running smoothly, you get congratulated.

As a process engineer and production manager at Gorton's of Gloucester, I tracked the asset utilization and efficiency on every production line in the plant. I produced one efficiency number that the plant manager and vice president could look at first thing in the morning to see how the plant had run the day before. If the plant ran at 95 percent for the day, I would expect an "Attaboy!" If it ran at 72 percent, I expected a "What the hell happened?"

So, back to real estate—what the heck does all this production talk have to do with that? Well, if you have purchased a real estate investment that earns income when it's occupied, it probably makes sense to track it, right?

So, let's look at my Isalene property. So far this year it looks like this:

- Weekly rentals—8 weeks booked so far this season = 56 days

- Weekend rentals—3 long weekends = 9 days

- My vacation—2 weeks = 14 days

- My long weekends—20 x 3 days = 60 days

- Total usage = 139 days

Well, there are 365 days in a year, so that's 139/365 = 38 percent asset utilization.

Chapter 10 – Investing And Saving

Not very good, right? There's room for improvement! I'll work on that!

So, when I increase the asset utilization, more money will come in and I can pay off the house quicker! Before long, I will be sipping margaritas in Florida and enjoying the Cape during the warm summer months of Massachusetts. Real estate can be an excellent investment. I love this particular investment the most, because it is a house I never want to sell. I would be very comfortable living there for whatever amount of time I decide.

When looking at a real estate investment, I believe it is important to ask yourself: "Could I live here comfortably for the rest of my life if I had to?" Or, if it is an investment that you know you are planning to sell in five to ten years, are you prepared for the ups and downs of the market, along with unexpected maintenance costs? Are you prepared to handle all the issues that can arise when dealing with tenants? As with all investments, do your homework!

Now, let's talk saving. When I moved back to Boston, I knew it would be just a matter of time before I relocated back to Fort Lauderdale. So why not save for those relocation costs? Sure, I might end up getting a job down there at a company that would pay for those costs. But just to be sure, why don't I save some money, just in case?

With my part-time bartending job, I promised myself that I would put twenty dollars for every shift I worked into an envelope for my relocation to Florida. If I earned over two hundred dollars for the shift, I would save forty dollars. And if it was over three hundred dollars, I would save sixty dollars. I have been home now for about three and a half years, and that envelope has over five thousand dollars cash in it. I get excited putting money into the envelope; I know it will be going to a great cause.

That's the trick: make saving, investing, and watching your money grow fun and exciting! Have a plan; calculate a specific amount that you want to save each month. When you have a plan, it also allows Tonto to assist you with sticking to it! When you can increase your contribution into your 401k though your company to 4, 5, 6, or 7 percent and so on, that's great. If you don't have a 401k through your company, you can start an individual retirement plan (IRA) through any of several accredited companies that you can find on the Internet.

Most important, when thinking of investing, do not forget about investing in your own personal education in the field that will benefit the most people and elevate your career!

An investment in knowledge pays the best interest.

—Benjamin Franklin

Chapter 11 – Equity and Debt

In 2008, countless people saw the equity in their homes vanish. The value of my three houses dropped by around $200,000 in one year. Can you imagine losing $200,000? Prior to this, the housing market had steadily increased, and it appeared to be a much better investment than the stock market. But when the housing bubble burst, one of my staff members had to go through the foreclosure process. He lost his house due to its drop in value.

I would like to share the story of how my equity disappeared. In 2001, I bought my first house for $245,000. I had always rented up to this point. The house's value quickly started to rise. I had bought at the right time. In only eight months, people started telling me my house was worth over $300,000. After one year, house sales in the area were averaging $350,000. Again people were telling me I had $100,000 equity in my house.

I thought this was fantastic! So what did I do? I went and bought another house. I bought one down on Cape Cod, Hyannis, for $182,000 in 2002. I always loved the Cape and rented a house there every summer, so that just made sense to me.

And guess what happened—the housing market continued to soar! In another year's time, my real estate agent told me that the Cape house had $100,000 equity. I was like, "You have to be kidding me. This is easy! I've been working my ass off and investing in my 401k for seventeen years, and I now have as much equity in my two houses as I do in my 401k!"

Now, don't forget: that $200,000 vanished!

I did not know the housing market was going to crash, so I kept buying. I borrowed money from the equity on my first house to buy another house down the Cape. This time, I bought in West Hyannisport, close to beautiful Craigville beach. I bought this one in 2004 for $295,000.

The market would continue to rise for about one more year. At one point around this time, I asked my agent a question: "If I put my other Cape house on the market right now, what would you suggest for an asking price?" She said $315,000. I had paid $182,000 for that house. But I did not put it on the market at that time, which was the peak of the housing market. Well, it would have been a very smart move if I had! If you learn from my decision, and I hope you will, that would make me happy.

Instead, I added up all the appraised values of my three homes and got $1.1 million. Here I was, at around forty years of age, owning over a million dollars in property. I thought I was king. I owed around $750,000 in mortgages. So I thought the $350,000 in equity was mine to spend however I wanted. I did not look at it as being three quarters of a million dollars in debt; I looked at it as owning over a million dollars in property. I took out home equity loans and credit cards for home improvement projects. I took trips, and I spent money on things I really didn't need. I also made that career change I talked about but didn't change my spending habits.

I took some of those so-called great credit card deals with 0 percent interest for the first year. Before I knew it, I had a Chase credit card with a $16,000 balance and a Capital One credit card with a $24,000 balance. Granted, most of the money I spent with those cards was on needed repairs and improvements on my houses, like a new roof and a new bathroom.

Chapter 11 – Equity And Debt

I was under the impression that if I put money into my real estate investments, I would get it back plus more when the property was sold. This is not always the case. Many people got burned after the housing bubble because they borrowed from the equity in their homes to build additions and make other home improvements. Then they realized they couldn't afford the new mortgage payment with the economy going into a depression.

I finally woke up and realized that I could not pay all the bills and mortgages that were coming in. So I called my real estate agent back and said, "Hey, I believe I need to put that house on the market now."

She said, "OK, but the market has changed drastically, and you will be lucky to make your money back on that house." Unfortunately, there were five other houses also for sale on that street, all at lower prices than I wanted to ask.

The bubble burst, the bottom fell out—however you want to put it, I was in trouble.

When I realized I was over my head with mortgage payments, credit lines, credit cards, and bills, I added up all my debt. It was $780,000. That was four years ago. Today, my total debt is $680,000. I have reduced it by $100,000 in four years. That is $25,000 per year, and I still have my three houses.

Now, there are people out there, intelligent people, who would say I would have been better off declaring bankruptcy. That would have erased all my credit cards and given me a fresh start to begin living normally again. But the reality is, I borrowed that money, and I want to pay it all back. I am a man of solid integrity. I did not borrow to buy drugs or do anything illegal. It was for home improvement projects.

Now I know: don't spend money I don't have!

The lesson to be learned here is, be careful with equity. It can vanish overnight. Avoid debt!

> When you get in debt, you become a slave.
>
> —Andrew Jackson

The quickest way to financial freedom is to pay off all your debts.

You can read stories of "good" debt and "bad" debt, but they are really the same—you owe money, and you have to pay it off, almost always with interest.

A great task to do is write down all the debt you have—every financial institution, bank, company, organization, or person that you owe money to. Then calculate when all these debts will be paid off. This is an eye-opening exercise that could work like a slap in the face, a little reality check. It did for me; I thought I was wealthier than I really was.

But you can turn it around and get excited about reducing debt and getting financially free. And then it can become fun!

One financial number I currently track (and you might want to) is how much I reduce my debt plus how much I increase my savings each year. I update the numbers every month to see where I stand. So for example, halfway through this year, my financial number is $45,457. I have reduced my debt by $14,947, and my savings have gone up $30,510.

Now, that's a pretty sweet number. If I am at roughly $45,000 in July, I could be at $90,000 by December. God willing, I have about fifteen years to retirement. So if I multiply fifteen years by $90,000, it equals $1.35 million. You see? That's how it can be fun.

Chapter 11 – Equity And Debt

The $30,510 savings increase in six months is not typical for the amount of money I have in my savings plan. It has been a very good year for the stock market. There have actually been some negative numbers in years past, and there will probably be some more negative numbers in the future.

But the exciting thing is the amount of debt decreasing. You actually have more control over debt than you do the savings! Look at your statements; you can see the amount of debt (principal) and the amount of interest you pay each month.

It is important to analyze all your debts and prioritize which ones you are going to pay off first, usually based on the highest interest rates. An example: I know I want to pay off one of my Cape Cod houses as soon as possible. So any additional money that comes my way, or that I can save, I put toward that debt. I also realize that if I am paying a $200 credit card bill at a much higher interest rate, it makes more sense to pay that off first. Once I am free from that credit card debt, I will take that $200 per month and put it toward the principal on my Cape house.

One of my current goals is to practice frugality and reduce debt wherever possible! And unless I win the lottery, it will always be one of my goals. I do not play the lottery, so that won't happen. I do not gamble, because I want to become a self-made millionaire the old fashioned way—by earning it! Regarding debt, I believe Thomas Jefferson said it best:

Never spend your money before you have it.

Chapter 12 – Frugality

If you practice frugality, it could be the best way to find financial freedom. Frugality is often defined as "finding and embracing cost-free options."

Last summer, my brother Dan and I climbed a mountain in the beautiful White Mountains of New Hampshire. It was the first mountain I had climbed. This mountain is home of the famous Indian Head, and it is called Mount Pemigewasset. It is not a huge mountain—one and a half miles to the top and a little over twenty-five hundred feet. The view from up top is amazing!

Chapter 12 – Frugality

Now how much did it cost to climb the mountain? Zero. I did have some trail mix, beef jerky, water, and a couple Coors Light cans in my backpack. So if we want to get technical, I spent about $7.50 on food and drinks.

At times on this hike, my body felt like it was on a Stairmaster Stepmill. This piece of cardio equipment burns a lot of calories, and it can be found at many gyms. Mountain climbing and hiking are an excellent, low-cost option for fun, exercise, and sightseeing.

I wish I had learned about practicing frugality years ago. Most people spend money based on what they earn. If they earn one hundred thousand dollars per year, that's a good amount of money; they should buy all the things they want, right?

The key to financial freedom is to analyze all that you spend and reduce expenditures in areas that don't add value. I love Starbucks coffee. I would love to stop by Starbucks each morning on my way to work like millions of other people do. (OK, the other people actually stop at Dunkin' Donuts.) I know that if I brew a cup of coffee with my single-cup brewer at the house, though, it costs me about $0.05 compared to $2.00 at Starbucks. That is over a 97.5 percent savings!

There are so many avenues for spending less and saving more, it's ridiculous. Look for free options! Barter for some of your work! Shop around for the best prices, especially with food. I look though the advertisements that come in the mail and find great deals. I can get good lean protein and vegetables at three different locations at great prices: boneless chicken breast and center-cut pork chops for under $2.00 a pound and bananas for $0.49 a pound.

Take a serious look at your food bill—you know, that slip you get at the grocery market. When you look at it closely, two thoughts will come up: One: *I know I could have bought this elsewhere at a lower* price. Two: *I know I just purchased some items that are not in line with my fitness goals.*

Earlier, I mentioned people who say, "Hey, just focus and work harder, and you will get that extra money. Then you won't be perceived as frugal, cheap, and a penny pincher, and other terms like that. (Where the heck did that phrase come from, anyway? You can't pinch a penny—it's copper. And I'm pretty sure the penny won't feel it.)

I read something a little while ago that told me I might be on to something here: most millionaires shop at Walmart, and many of them will go to the dollar store for certain items. A millionaire at a dollar store—does that make any sense? Yes. In fact, it makes a lot of *cents*. How do you think they became millionaires? Most millionaires buy used cars that get good gas mileage and live in smaller homes for longer periods of time.

In my manufacturing career, I was introduced to the terms *lean thinking* and *value stream mapping*. These two topics yield valuable information that can benefit you for the rest of your life. The terms were never defined for me as "being frugal with your inventory or manufacturing process," but that is pretty much exactly what they are.

Lean thinking is working with your suppliers to get the best price for the exact quantity you need for a specific time frame.

Value stream mapping is looking at your process and identifying piles of inventory that negatively affect your cash flow.

Now let's look at some real-life lean-thinking examples you can apply at home.

For my small household of one, I go to the dollar store and spend ten dollars on cleaning supplies for one month. I buy laundry detergent,

Chapter 12 – Frugality

dish detergent, antibacterial surface cleaner, soap, shampoo, trash bags, sandwich bags, antiperspirant, toothpaste, and mouthwash for ten bucks!

If I bought those products at the local supermarket, pharmacy, or building center, they would probably cost me twenty-five to thirty dollars. If you take the money saved and invest it into a good savings plan, it could provide some nice additional cash.

Here is the math: $20 per month times twelve months = $240 per year. If you put $240 per year into an investment account that earned 8 percent interest between ages thirty and sixty-five, that would yield $44,905.

That's not a bad return. And who cares if you are not in your thirties? This type of savings still works in your forties, fifties, and sixties. We are all planning on living to one hundred, so it's never too late to start saving.

That was just one small example of saving twenty bucks a month—I bet you could think of a dozen more ideas. I used to get my oil changed in my car at a place that charged me $55.00, and now I go to one that charges me $17.95. That is a savings of $37.05.

What if we added these extra bucks to our mortgage payments and paid off our houses quicker? Not a bad investment for those bucks.

Here are some at-home value stream mapping examples:

I enjoy timing things perfectly to run out just after a backup is purchased. So, for example, I pull out the last piece of tinfoil just after I purchase a backup roll two days earlier. It's kind of like a game for me. I win if I get perfect timing. You can do this with everything: toothpaste, paper towels, sandwich bags, and food.

This improves cash flow and reduces clutter around the house. If you need to go a few days without something, so what? You improvise or find another way. If it's an emergency, go get it. There is a twenty-four-hour CVS half a mile from my house. If it's an emergency and I need to get something, I actually get a little excited because I get to run down to CVS and back. This nice one-mile run adds an extra workout for the day. Now, I know my thinking is a little strange, and most people might not get excited about going for a mile run in the middle of the night. But what the heck? Even just walking one mile to clear the head, get some fresh air, and save a little gas is great!

Let me share a story with you. (And please, Mom, don't get mad at me.) My mom and dad went shopping every Friday. It really became the big event for the week; it was their routine. They went each Friday for those certain items they had to buy each week.

When my mom went up to heaven and my dad to the nursing home, we kids had the task of cleaning out their place. One closet had so many boxes of tissues, you could have built a small house with them. (Again, sorry, Mom. It's a good example that can help people; you always like to help people.) My brother Dan took the tissues out of the closet and stacked the boxes in front of the apartment complex (yep, he built a small house). Then he put up a sign that said Help Yourself, and they were gone quickly.

My parents had a six-month supply of many items. You probably can take a look around your house and find a number of things that you purchased and might not need for a while.

Companies that do not practice these principles—they don't get the best price from their supplier, and they buy the incorrect quantity and thus carry piles of inventory—usually go out of business and/or file bankruptcy. Sometimes it is helpful to look at your household spending

Chapter 12 – Frugality

like you are running a company. This company you want dearly to be profitable, not to go out of business or declare bankruptcy.

Frugality, lean thinking, and value stream mapping are three concepts that can help improve your financial situation if you practice them.

> Frugality is one of the most beautiful and joyful words in the English language, and yet one that we are culturally cut off from understanding and enjoying. The consumption society has made us feel that happiness lies in having things, and has failed to teach us the happiness of not having things.
>
> —Elise Boulding

Chapter 13 – Family

There is no sum of money that I would trade for the relationships I have with my family. I am not married and do not have any kids, so I am talking about my parents, my brothers, my sister, my nieces and nephews, my sisters-in-law, and my brother-in-law.

I cannot understand people who do not get along with family members and hold grudges and haven't talked to them in years. You might say I'm just lucky or that none of my family members ever did anything bad to me. But I believe it was the way our parents brought us up. We are very tight. I would do anything to help out my family members, and I believe they all would do the same.

I spent Easter at my brother Marty and his wife Darlene's place. Most of our family was there, and we had a fantastic time. We watched some great NCAA basketball, chatted away on various topics, reminisced about the Easters we shared growing up, and ate some fantastic food. My brother Danny brought over six racks of lamb, a leg of lamb, and a bunch of other food, so no one left hungry. My parents used to provide the best holiday meals a kid could ask for. That might be why I love and enjoy food so much.

Did we always get along this well? No. We fought a lot when we were younger. I think that's normal, though.

I had a great weekend in October with my brothers Marty and Danny. I asked them for some help getting my Saint Joseph Street property ready for the market. The tenant who had lived in the house

Chapter 13 – Family

for the past five years had just moved out. The bathroom was a mess, and the grout and caulking around the tub was black instead of its original white. The house needed cleaning, and we needed to do a lot of landscaping maintenance.

The three of us worked hard and banged out the needed work. Marty made the bathroom look like new; he's a talented machine when it comes to tile work. He even dug out the grout in the floor and put in a new, awesome color. Danny and I put together a patio with pavers, and we cleaned up the yard for some good curb appeal. We made the house look so good, the next people who came to look at it put in an offer. And we ended up agreeing on a price.

Having brothers who will jump in and help me when I need them is priceless. Yes, I will get a few bucks back when the house finally closes, but like I said, no dollar amount could replace the relationship I have with them.

Five years ago I decided to relocate to Fort Lauderdale, Florida. I always loved that area, and I was a little tired of long winters and shoveling snow. My brother Andy and his wife, Kim, were living in Coral Springs, right outside Fort Lauderdale. They had a beautiful four-bedroom house with a swimming pool. They had invited me many times to move down and said they had a bedroom with my name on it. They might not have thought I would actually take them up on their offer, but I did.

It was a fantastic time. Of course, they're my brother and sister-in-law, but they are also some of my best friends. We had a blast living together. I can vividly recall hearing the blender going as I pulled in the driveway each Friday evening. Kim was very timely making the margaritas on Friday night. They are such cool people that the neighborhood folks would always come over on the weekend to join the party—such a good time.

Then Andy got a new job in Denver, Colorado, and they relocated. That was OK; they got to live in and experience another beautiful place in our country. By then I was well established, so I rented a nice one-bedroom condo right off Fort Lauderdale beach. I lived in that condo for a year and had an awesome time.

If I had not had the relationship with my brother and his wife, that whole great experience probably wouldn't have happened. Like I mentioned earlier, strong family relations is priceless.

In the summers, my sister Pam and her family always travel to the Cape, where we do a nice family vacation. Most of the family shows up during the week, and we have a blast. We have created many awesome family memories there, and we will continue that tradition for years to come.

Last month, I watched my niece Lauren win the cup in her division playing college soccer. She was captain and Most Valuable Player of the team. I am so proud to be an uncle and/or a godfather to my nieces and nephews! They are terrific kids and young adults, and their parents have done a fantastic job raising them.

So if you have not talked with a family member for a while because of something that happened a while ago, give a call or go visit. Apologize even if you feel you were not in the wrong. I'll bet you ten bucks the reply will be, "No, it was my fault," or "I was wrong too." Life is too short to hold grudges. Cherish your family relationships!

Family is not an important thing; it's everything.

—Michael J. Fox

Chapter 14 – The Importance of a Strong Work Ethic

This chapter is about my dad.

The value of a strong work ethic is underrated. I don't think it is taught in school. I believe it is something you acquire from your family and the friends you choose to hang with. I believe my strong work ethic comes from my dad.

I can recall when he first asked me to work for him on the weekend. My dad was running a catering company at this time. I said, "Sure, I would love to."

He said, "Great, I could use your help this Saturday."

He woke me up at 5:30 a.m., and we were on the road by 6:00 a.m. We drove up to Lowell, Massachusetts, about an hour away. We spent the morning prepping food for the big party that night; it was a wedding. I spent the afternoon loading the trucks with food, plates, chafing dishes, and all the necessary equipment for the party. Then we drove to the event and unloaded the trucks. We set up for the party, and then we ran the party. Once it was over, we had to break down the party and load up the trucks. Then we drove back to his company and unloaded all the equipment and leftover food. We also washed some of the equipment we had used. Then we drove back home, arriving around 12:30 a.m. We had worked a nineteen-hour day, including the commute. He said to me, "There, son, now that's a day's work!" My dad worked these types of days all the time. Once in a while, he would say, "Look, kids, I only worked half a day today—twelve hours."

A few years later, he asked me if I wanted to get into the catering business. I said, "Are you crazy? That's freaking tough work!"

I like what General Colin Powell said: "There are no secrets to success; hard work, persistence, and loyalty to those whom you work for are the keys to success."

My dad had an awesome career, and I am so proud of him. He went to Cornell University and received his degree in hotel and restaurant management in 1953. He did his internship at the Ritz Carlton in Boston, where he started learning about premier food service. He went on to hold those positions I mentioned earlier: director of food service at Rutgers University, Boston University, and Lowell University. Then he ran his own catering business for years.

My brothers, sister, and I were sure glad he chose the food business; we never had to worry about going hungry. We did often wonder whether we had so many friends growing up because they actually liked us or because we had so much food in the house.

Our dad is a special person. When we were growing up in Nahant, Massachusetts, he did something unique and inspiring. On Thanksgiving morning, he would wake up at 2:00 a.m. and start making donuts for the neighborhood. He made cinnamon, sugar, and plain donuts, along with donut holes. When we woke up, our job was to deliver them and thank people for being such good neighbors. He called it "the Pilgrim Bakeshop." Who does that kind of thing?

Even though my dad worked very long hours, he was always there to support us kids in our sports activities and other achievements in

Chapter 14 – The Importance Of A Strong Work Ethic

life. For my younger brothers, Marty, Andy and Danny, he was their Little League coach. The team was called the Orioles, and they had a great time. They won the championship his last year coaching them. He was so proud of that bright-orange championship jacket that he wore it all the time for many years following.

Our dad provided the most unbelievable place for us kids to grow up. It was a big, five-bedroom, four-bathroom house right on the ocean in beautiful Nahant, Massachusetts. I am so grateful for that and could not have asked for a better place to spend my childhood. He bought us a boat with lobster traps, and I spent the summers fishing and catching lobsters. I absolutely loved it. I found out I could actually make some money selling the lobsters if I could get them by my mom and sister…

Tonight, I was sitting with my dad at Life Care on the North Shore. I shared with him what I have written so far about him. With his dementia, I am not sure how much of it he really comprehended. When I mentioned some things, like him working at the Ritz Carlton and the Pilgrim Bakeshop, he smiled and even chuckled a bit. They say that with dementia, the further back you go with events, the more likely it is that people remember.

So then I asked him, "Dad, what accomplishments are you most proud of in your life?" He stared at me, trying to think; all that came out was silence.

It makes me think. Tonto yells into my ear, "Tom, you dope! Why did you not have these conversations with him years ago? Or with your mother?" I wish I knew what they were most proud of. I also wanted to know the mistakes they made so I could learn from them. So, if your parents and grandparents are still alive, if you haven't already, have those conversations with them. Someday they won't be here, and you might regret not learning more about them!

This past weekend, I was visiting my dad, and I said to him with excitement, "Dad, I am writing a book, and I have a hundred and forty pages written so far! Isn't that great?"

He gave a little smile and said, "Yeah, that's great!"

I asked him, "How many copies of the book do you think I will sell?"

He thought for a minute, held up his right hand, making a peace sign, and said, "Two."

I smiled and then thought, *If I sell four books, that would be double my dad's expectations. That is what's really important to me!* When you have exceeded the expectations of the people who mean the most to you, you are truly successful.

Exceeding people's expectations applies to family, friends, your coworkers, and your customers. It does not matter what line of work you are in, someone will always have certain expectations from you.

If you are a waiter or waitress, people will come into your establishment and expect good service. When you exceed their expectations, it makes them very happy, which in turn makes you happy and will normally be reflected in the tip.

If you are a contractor, the same principle applies. You go into a house for some repair work, and the customer has certain expectations. When you go over and above what they expected, only good things can come of it. If you work for a company, your boss expects certain things from you. Exceeding these things only sets you up for a promotion or other types of rewards.

Chapter 14 – The Importance Of A Strong Work Ethic

My dad loved watching football! He loved the Green Bay Packers when they had players like Bart Starr and when Vince Lombardi was the coach. Perhaps that's where he acquired some of his wisdom. Vince Lombardi, I believe, had a very strong work ethic:

> The dictionary is the only place where success comes before work. Hard work is the price we must pay for success. I think you can accomplish anything if you're willing to pay the price.
>
> —Vince Lombardi

Thank you, Dad, for all that you taught me!

Chapter 15 – The Energizer Bunny

This chapter is about my mom.

This weekend, it will be Mother's Day. It will be my second Mother's Day without my mom; she went up to heaven on February 5, 2011, after an eight-year battle with cancer. The people at the Mass General North Shore Cancer Center called her "The Energizer Bunny" because she keep going and going.

When I think of my mom, I think of integrity and good, solid values. The word *integrity* comes from a Latin word meaning "whole, complete." It suggests qualities such as honesty and consistency of character. Demonstrating *good, solid values* means teaching us right from wrong, being honest, and always doing the right thing.

I can recall, at age twelve or thirteen, going shopping with my mom. She took me to a Star Market supermarket in Lynn, Massachusetts. It wasn't one of the best neighborhoods in the country, if you know what I mean. We were pulling out of the parking lot when she felt our car hit the car next to us, although she had barely touched the other car. We got out to see if there was any damage but could not see any. We got back into the car, and she pulled out a piece of paper and a pen, and started writing. I said, "Mom, what are you doing?"

She said, "I am going to leave a note on their windshield with my name and number in case I did some damage."

Chapter 15 – The Energizer Bunny

I said, "No one saw us. I can't see any damage. We're in Lynn, so just take off!"

She said, "No, son, that would not be the right thing to do!" She taught us to do the right thing in all circumstances—a valuable lesson I will never forget.

My mom spent most of her life raising us kids. She had seven, but one passed away at a very young age, before I was born. We never talked that much about him. He was my brother Stephen, whom I never met. Perhaps I will meet him in an afterlife. It had to be devastating for my mom to lose a child.

When I look back on all the work she did raising my four brothers, my sister, and me, I think, *Wow, she did so much!* Laundry, dinners, lunches, breakfasts, rides to events, cleaning our big house with four bathrooms, and on and on. I didn't appreciate it back then as much as I should have. We were the kind of brats who would say things like, "Hey, Mom, my baseball uniform is still dirty! What do you mean you didn't wash it?" What an asshole I was.

I remember she took me to a car dealership, let me pick out a car, and rented it for me so I could drive to my senior prom in a nice, new, fancy car. What a cool mom. She did many things like that for us.

My mom won a lot of beauty pageants growing up, and we can thank her for passing on some of those good looks. Many of us kids were voted best looking in junior high and high school. Thanks, Mom!

How my mom and dad met was classic. She was living on the West Coast, in Oregon, and she was engaged to be married. Before she got married, though, she decided to take a little time for herself and come out to the East Coast and visit with her sister Nornie in Connecticut.

My Aunt Nornie convinced my mom to stay for New Year's Eve and actually fixed her up with a blind date for the night. That was the first time my dad met my mom. She never went back to the West Coast! They got married and spent fifty-three fantastic years together.

My mom was a great cook, and she made the best lobster bakes on the planet. She would serve fifteen to twenty lobsters, clams, mussels, corn on the cob, potatoes, and awesome chicken wings. I am not sure how she made those wings so amazing. I know she cooked them halfway in the oven and then parboiled them so the meat just fell of the bone. We had plenty of hot, melted butter for dipping, and we would eat for hours. Those were some of the best days!

And the holidays—forget about it! I believe we had some of the best holidays possible. For Easter, we had baskets at our beds filled to the brim, the dining room table was covered with treats, and she served a fabulous dinner. For Christmas, we found a ridiculous amount of gifts under the big, gorgeous, real tree, and she served a huge prime rib, always cooked to perfection. Our mom made sure every holiday was terrific, with no exceptions!

Although she sounds like the angel she was, she laid down the law when it was the right thing to do!

My older brother, Chris, stepped out of line one time, and she punched him in the mouth! That diamond ring busted open his lip pretty good. That sure sent a message to the family. That was some of her advice: you run into a bully, just punch him right in the mouth.

Occasionally, while taking a shower, I will accidentally get a little soap in my mouth, and I'll be reminded of when I got my mouth

Chapter 15 – The Energizer Bunny

washed out with soap. When we swore as kids growing up, our mom would stick that whole bar in our mouths and really wash them good.

Today, kids get a "time-out." What the heck is that? When I was first introduced to this time-out thing. I was like, "What, you get to relax and just chill, and you don't have any disturbance around you? Wow, that's great!" Periodically, if I was around a bunch of kids for a long time, I would say, "Tom needs a time-out," and I would go relax for an hour or so.

You call that punishment? Ha. My dad's spankings, those were punishment. We were afraid of doing the wrong thing.

When my mom went up to heaven, my family asked me to do the eulogy at her funeral, and I agreed. This was a tough task. It was not the public speaking—I have done that in front of huge crowds—but it was tough because I was representing my family and did not want to disappoint them in any way.

I prepared the speech and practiced it by myself in my living room fifteen or twenty times the night before the event. It was only six and a half minutes long. I didn't sleep well that night before her Mass. I kept thinking, "Don't let down your family. You must deliver this talk flawlessly." I prayed endlessly to ask the Lord help me deliver a true representation of my mom's life on earth in this mere six-and-a-half-minute speech.

The Lord helped me out, and what I said came out very well, without a hitch or stumble. I am not sure whether or not it is appropriate to put a eulogy in a book. And I am brand-new at writing books; this is my first one. But I will share this with you because I believe these words will drive you to be a better person, guaranteed!

THOMAS EDWARD MUSER

My Mom's Eulogy: Carol Ann Muser

Carol Ann Muser, our mom, was born Carol Ann Lindstrom in Tacoma, Washington. She grew up in Redmond, Oregon. Fifty-five years ago, she came out here to visit her sister in Connecticut. On that visit, she met our dad on a blind date on New Year's Eve. They got married soon after and spent fifty-three wonderful years together.

She was truly a beautiful person inside and outside. She won many beauty contests growing up; however, inside she was more beautiful.

She spent most of her life raising us kids and teaching us great values, ethics, and integrity.

I would like to share with you a short story that displays her teachings:

A few years ago, my brother Marty, my brother Danny, and I went on a trip to British Columbia. We were celebrating Marty's birthday, and this was a place he always wanted to see.

I recall the flight home. It was around six and a half hours. When we landed in Boston and were ready to dock, one of the flight attendants came back to our row. She stopped and looked at the three of us and said, "Are you all brothers?"

Naturally, we thought we had done something wrong. We said, "Yes, we are brothers."

Chapter 15 – The Energizer Bunny

She said, "The other flight attendants and I were talking, and we were so impressed by how polite you all were—how you said please and thank you every time we came by with something."

As she was telling us this, her voice got louder, as if she was sending a message to the other people on the plane. Perhaps they weren't that polite, did not say please and thank you, and might have even been rude.

She then looked at us and said, "Your mom did a fantastic job raising you boys! I must repeat that: Your mom did a fantastic job raising you boys!" And that, she did!

A few years back, our mom wrote a poem to us kids, and I would like to share that with you today:

To My Children—Luv, Mom

I Love You All!

I have given you my life, and you have given me so much joy, and not to mention a wee bit of woe. I pray and hope that life gives you all that you hope for, and never disappoints you, but gives even more.

I believe in destiny, and you must choose what your path in life will be. Your bedmates and partners will influence your life, but you must never be deterred from what you believe in and what you must do with the rest of your life.

You must keep faith in God and what you feel in your heart and do what is most important to you and the people who live around you.

This is a very powerful poem. We will think of it when faced with challenges and decisions we must make, and she will continue to guide us in the right direction.

She was a true fighter right to the end. She battled cancer for eight years. She had six surgeries, had to eat through a tube in her stomach for over a year, and went through countless radiation and chemo treatments. Toward the end, she was given experimental medication, new chemo treatments, and new technology. The doctors said they didn't know how the experimental treatments would work, but the experiments might help other people.

She said, "If it will help other people, let's go for it!" At the Mass General Cancer Center, her tenacity and her desire to not give up earned her the nickname, "Energizer Bunny." She just kept going and going, right up till her last week at the Hospice House in Danvers, Massachusetts. They told us on a Monday night that she had one to two days left, maybe only hours. Five days later, she was still with us. The hospice staff looked at her, saying, "Wow. She's amazing."

Mom, you are a true inspiration to everyone. We are so grateful for all that you taught us, and all the love you gave us!

Chapter 15 – The Energizer Bunny

We will do our best to make you proud and cherish the memories you created.

Rest now, Mom. You deserve it. We will love you forever.

My dad wanted a few things said on this day:

Dad's words:

> *To my wife—*
>
> *I never heard a bad word said about you, and that is very special.*
>
> *You never ever complained about not having enough money, and that is rare.*
>
> *I will miss your smile and having you by my side.*
>
> *You made my life complete.*
>
> *Heaven is now whole with your presence.*
>
> *You made sure we had our last rites read so that one day we would be together again.*
>
> *I love you and miss you!*

Chapter 16 – Friends

How many times have you heard of someone you knew or grew up with that got into serious trouble—maybe with drugs, stealing, drinking, or something else illegal? And when someone is asked what happened to that person, the response is, "Well, she just got mixed up with the wrong people," or "He hung around with the wrong crowd."

The people you choose to spend time with can play a huge role in how far you get in life with your abilities and talents.

So, how do you know if you are hanging with the right people? It's very easy. You only need to ask yourself one question: do they help move you toward achieving your goals, or do they move you away from achieving them?

Sure, there are other factors too: Are they positive or negative? Are they optimistic or pessimistic? When you tell them about a goal you want to achieve, are they supportive and encouraging? Do they make you laugh and smile? Do you have fun when you hang with them? Or do you get into trouble?

I know there were times when I spent time with the wrong people and got into trouble, and their influence prevented me from using some of my abilities.

I had many great friends growing up, I still have great friends, and I plan on meeting more people who will turn out to be great friends.

Chapter 16 – Friends

Succeeding in life will not mean much if you don't have good friends to share your success with!

> My best friend is the one who brings out the best in me.
>
> —Henry Ford

Some of my closest friends right now are people I met in my bartending days at the Porthole Pub in Lynn, Massachusetts. Bredog and Pitdog are two that come to mind. (I'll use their nicknames to protect the guilty.) These two guys would come in a heartbeat if I needed their help.

Pitdog organizes a guys' weekend every year, among other events. He has done this for over twenty years. It's always a great time filled with plenty of friends, golf, cigars, beer, Grand Marnier, and tons of laughs.

If you have something like this going on in your life, fantastic! If not, perhaps you could become the organizer or delegate someone for that task, such as a friend who's good on Facebook and has great communication skills.

True friends are the ones you laugh with so hard that your stomach hurts the next day. Laughter releases endorphins, your feel-good chemicals, and I believe that feeling gets multiplied by the number of good friend that you are cracking up with.

> Laughter is a very strong medicine for the body and mind. Laughter is a powerful antidote to stress, pain, and conflict. Nothing works faster or more dependably to bring your mind and body back into balance

> than a good laugh. Humor lightens your burdens, inspires hopes, connects you to others, and keeps you grounded, focused, and alert.
>
> —Melinda Smith and Jeanne Segal

I have been extremely fortunate to have all the friends I do, and I will always cherish those relationships. I won't list them all in this book—you know who you are! They came from high school, college, my days at Gorton's, in Germany, in Florida, in my fitness career, and in my bartending career.

Tonto is my friend too! He is my inner voice; he's the one who gives me a dope slap or a kick in the gluteus maximus when I need it. He will say, "Get off your lazy ass and go get it done!" He is the one who makes sure I have the self-discipline to do what needs to be done, when it needs to be done, with no excuses. We all have this inner voice, and listening to it can be very beneficial. It can be a powerful motivator.

> Don't let the noise of others' opinions drown out your own inner voice.
>
> —Steve Jobs, Stanford University commencement speech, 2005

Chapter 17 – My Favorite Motivators and Role Models

As you travel down the path in life there will be people you look up to and admire. These people can inspire you and motivate you to get to the next level. I believe it is important to have role models that you can learn from. When you do what successful people do you too become successful!

I must start with sports figures I admired, and I would have to say that they were my first role models.

I admired Dr. J—Julius Erving of the Philadelphia 76ers.

His athletic ability to drive to the hoop and float through the air was amazing to watch. Playing basketball was my favorite thing to do when I was a kid, so watching Dr. J play was great! He is the fifth-highest-scoring player in basketball history, with over thirty thousand points. He was and still is a class act, both on and off the court.

The next person I idolized was Walter Payton.

He played for thirteen years in the NFL for the Chicago Bears and was known as "Sweetness." He was graceful and powerful. He was quick and consistent. He always gave 100 percent. In games today, some of the running backs run out of bounds before they get hit. But never Walter Payton! Defensive players coming up on Walter had to get prepared for the hit. And the way he always bounced up after the hit was amazing. He never did crazy celebrations after his touchdowns; he just handed the ball over to the ref.

His conditioning programs were top-notch, and it showed. In his book *Never Die Easy*, he described how his mother would have a truckload of dirt brought to his house in the beginning of the summer. She would have Walter and his brother move that dirt with shovels and wheelbarrows all over the yard all summer long. It kept him out of trouble and taught him about conditioning.

Mike Ditka called Walter Payton the greatest football player he had ever seen, and he said he was an even greater human being. Like Dr J, Walter was also a total class act.

Then there was Michael Jordan. When he first came along, I said, "This guy is good, but he won't take over the top spot as my favorite basketball player." Well, over the years—sorry, Doc—Michael is just plain ridiculous with a basketball.

I believe MJ is the greatest basketball player of all time. He is phenomenal both on and off the court. He is still one of the most successfully marketed athletes in the world. He has been out of the NBA for years and still earned over seventy million dollars last year, most from advertising.

Lou Holtz was one of the first motivational speakers I heard, and I loved what he presented and his philosophies on life.

I really love and believe in Lou Holtz's three rules of life:

1. *Do the right thing.* To me this means, when faced with decisions in life, just ask yourself what is truly the right thing to do in that situation. Which decision offers the most integrity? You can even ask God or your parents, "What would you want me to do with this choice I have in life?" Just do the right thing!

Chapter 17 – My Favorite Motivators And Role Models

2. *Do your very best.* I believe this means don't do anything half-assed. If you are doing a job or completing a task, do it to the best of your abilities. Or don't do it at all!

3. *Treat other people like you want to be treated* (also known as the Golden Rule). This rule has helped me so much throughout my careers. Whenever I was faced with delivering disciplinary action or corrective action, I always put myself in the other person's shoes and said it how would I want it explained to me.

Tonto always back ups these three rules and reinforces them!

Lou believes that by following these three rules, you can grow your self-confidence, and you don't need to worry about being a good person. There is a Lou Holtz statue at Notre Dame with three words written on the bottom: Trust, Commitment, and Love. His players came up with those three words, which represent Lou's core values.

Earl Nightingale is another favorite motivator whom I have learned from. He was called "the dean of personal development." He was the first person to sell over a million copies of a spoken-word recording: *The Strangest Secret.* This strangest secret is that we become what we think about. This is so true—in my last year working at Gorton's of Gloucester, all I kept thinking about was doing personal training. I would be sitting in a meeting, not paying attention to the topic on hand, just picturing myself at a gym and taking people through workouts. This was not fair to the company, and it wasn't fair to me. Sure enough, I became what I thought about, and I have been training people for ten years now.

Earl published an audio program called *Lead the Field*, one of the most beneficial self-help tools I have purchased. This is an awesome program that I still listen to today. I have listened to his first recording, called "Attitude," hundreds of times, and it has contributed to my ability to always have a positive attitude.

Brian Tracy and Zig Ziglar also have been excellent motivators for me. They both have outstanding audio programs and books available in many areas of self-improvement.

The website www.nightingale.com is an excellent resource for audio programs. You will find all sorts of topics covered by some of the best motivators in the world. Listening to motivational CDs while driving instead of listening to the radio can change your life.

One of my clients told me about a book he read that changed his life. Based on the magnitude of success that my client has achieved, I said to myself, "You must read that book." The name of the book is *The Greatest Salesman in the World*, by Og Mandino. This book describes ten ancient scrolls that contain the secrets of getting the most out of life. I loved the book and the scrolls so much that I typed up a document with the titles of the ten scrolls and put it on my refrigerator. I look at it many times each day. What are those ten scrolls?

1. Today I begin my new life.

2. I will greet this day with love in my heart.

3. I will persist until I succeed.

4. I am nature's greatest miracle.

5. I will live this day as if it was my last.

6. Today I will be the master of my emotions.

Chapter 17 – My Favorite Motivators And Role Models

7. I will laugh at the world.

8. Today I will multiply my value a hundredfold.

9. I will act now, I will act now, I will act now.

10. I will pray for guidance.

Count your blessings. Once you realize how valuable you are and how much you have going for you, the smiles will return, the sun will break out, the music will play, and you will finally be able to move forward the life that God intended for you with grace, strength, courage, and confidence.

—Og Mandino

Chapter 18 – Faith in God

Today is a Sunday, and I did go to church this morning. My parents took us kids to church every Sunday morning when we were growing up. We said prayers before every meal, and we hit our knees every night before we went to bed and prayed. That is how we were brought up.

I must be honest—there were long periods of time when I did not attend Mass on Sundays, and many times I didn't hit my knees at night or say a prayer before I ate. I am not perfect!

When I was living with my brother Andy and his wife, Kim, down in Florida, there was a church down the street from them called Church by the Glades. The motto at the church is, "No perfect people allowed." I fit in well there. This is a great church that plays awesome music and always takes something out of the Bible and compares it to day-to-day life situations to help you make the right decisions.

This morning I attended the 10:30 a.m. Mass at St. Mary's of Danvers, Massachusetts. This is where my mother and father attended Mass up until she went up to heaven. When I attend Mass at St. Mary's, I can envision her sitting in the same seat, feel her presence, and see her smile, letting me know she is happy that I am there.

When I pray, there are four things I usually talk to God about. And if you do not believe in God, that's cool. We are each entitled to our own beliefs; that's what makes this country great. So you could just as easily say that these are four things that I meditate on or just think about:

Chapter 18 – Faith In God

1. Thank you, God, for the beautiful family I have: my mom up in heaven; my dad currently at Life Care; my brother Chris and his family; my sister Pam and her family; my brother Marty and his family; my brother Andy and his wife, Kim, down in Florida; and my brother Dan up in New Hampshire. Thank you also for all the great friends that I have, like Bredog and Pitdog.

2. I thank you, Lord, for being there for me. You are always there for me to talk to. Whether it is in a beautiful church or by my bedside, I know you are there to listen, and I thank you for that.

3. I want to thank you for my health. I am not sick, and I was able to work out today. There are so many people in the world that cannot physically or mentally work out like I did today. I really appreciate my fitness.

4. I want to thank you for all the success I have achieved in my life, and I ask you to keep me on this successful path. Please help me overcome the obstacles and events that try to throw me off track. May I utilize all the talents and gifts you have given me to make this world a better place. Amen.

This type of prayer makes me feel good inside. I think it is important to give thanks for all we have—not just on Thanksgiving Day, but every day.

Be grateful—take time to appreciate what you have.

Start with your physical abilities—your arms and your legs. Do you know how many people in the world are missing an arm, a leg, a hand, or a foot? Some people are born that way, some may have lost a limb in an accident, some have lost them serving our country proudly in the armed forces, and some have had amputations. I am truly grateful for my physical abilities, and I am aware that I must maintain and improve my physical abilities by working out regularly and eating right.

I am grateful for my mental abilities. The ability to use the human brain to think and make decisions is fantastic. Although sometimes my brain does not work as efficiently as I would like, it still works pretty good. I don't consider myself to be brilliant by any means. My brother Andy—now, he's brilliant. I like to think I'm smarter than the average bear.

Many people struggle with some type of brain disease or have disabilities and cannot do many things. So I am very fortunate that my mind still works and that I can keep learning. This world is so fascinating, and there is so much to learn. Never stop learning. When we stop learning, we die.

The human body is one of my favorite areas of study. I have acquired sixteen different certifications in the fitness industry, and I have learned quite a bit about how the human body works and the best ways to take care of it. But truthfully, I only know a tenth of what I want to know about the human body. One of my goals is to get another certification every year and/or attend a weekend fitness conference where I can increase my fitness knowledge.

I am grateful for the roof over my head and a warm house to live in. How many people in the world do not have adequate shelter from the elements? Recently we had a big storm in New England, and many people lost power and were without electricity and heat for up to five

Chapter 18 – Faith In God

days. Being without for any length of time gives people a new appreciation of a warm house. So I am very grateful to have the warm home that I presently sit in at a comfortable sixty-eight degrees, knowing that it is thirty-four degrees outside.

I am grateful for the food in my refrigerator and the food in my kitchen cabinets. I am thankful to have enough money to go food shopping each week. About twenty-one thousand people die each day from starvation; this is one person every four seconds. If you visit the website www.poverty.com, you can see the faces of these people. As I presently have four pounds of chicken breasts and a pound of whole wheat pasta cooking on the stove, I am very happy and grateful that I have food.

I am grateful to own my truck. It is not the nicest vehicle on the street; it is not a Porsche or a Mercedes. It is a 2007 Nissan Frontier with about eighty thousand miles on it. It is paid off and provides great transportation for me to go visit my dad and to visit my brother and his family, and it gets me to work Monday through Friday. Many people do not have a car and cannot afford one. I am thankful for my truck.

I am grateful for my two jobs. Many people are unemployed or underemployed. My jobs are the type that if I wanted to work more hours to earn more money, I could. That is rare.

To take the time and reflect on all the things you are truly grateful for makes you realize how cool this game of life is. It also makes you think. You have been given unique talents and gifts. Are you using them to their maximum potential?

We know we cannot do anything to change the past; we can only accept it, learn from it, and move on. Do not let it rent space in your head (as my good friend Darlene would say). It does not pay rent, so why should it stay there? That space is much too valuable; we need that space for knowledge, learning, and accomplishing our mission in life. We can influence and project our future, give 100 percent, and put the rest in God's hands. We can wake up each day with the mind-set to give our very best effort. Have faith in God, and he will help you overcome any obstacles or problems that come your way. God will guide us along the journey to completing a very successful life!

Chapter 19 – Mission Statement: Purpose in Life

My friend Phil Kaplan wrote a book that is called *The Best You've Ever Been*. He gave it to me to read because he was helping me improve my knowledge in the personal training industry. It is an excellent book! There is a chapter in it about writing your mission statement. After reading the chapter, I sat down with a pad of paper and wrote my mission statement. It was almost a page long, so I had to shorten it. I got it down to one big paragraph, and then finally to one sentence:

> I was put on this great planet earth to help people improve the quality of their life through fitness.

I do suggest taking the time to sit down and write your mission statement. What is it you were put on this planet to do? What are your special talents? What can you share with others? What gives you the greatest satisfaction? These are great questions that reveal a lot about what you should be doing with your life.

When I was in sixth grade, I received a special present for my birthday. It was the best present I have ever received. I can recall opening it like it was yesterday. I know where I opened it—in the library at our house in Nahant. I can still picture the yellow, black, and white shag rug on which the present sat. I can recall the wrapping paper—bright red, with snowmen on it. My birthday falls on December 31, right after Christmas. So, yes, it was Christmas wrapping paper.

The gift was very heavy; I could hardly move the box. I mentioned this gift earlier. It was a 115-pound barbell set. It had red-white-and-blue, plastic-coated cement plates in it, along with dumbbell bars and collars. The large barbell was also wrapped, and my dad brought it out after, because he thought the shape of it might give away the surprise of the present.

I was so happy, and I cannot think of another present that excited me that much. Inside the box, I unfolded a poster-sized diagram of the exercises that could be done with the weights. I tried all those exercises that day. Since that day, I have been experimenting with different workout programs. And I will continue to do so for the rest of my life.

The thrill I felt from this present was probably a hint that this was the line of work that I probably should go into. However, at age twelve, I was not thinking about my career.

This mission statement I still hold true today; I do believe I was put here on this planet to help people. I have helped many people achieve their fitness goals, and I plan to help many more.

The more I can increase my knowledge of how the human body works and the functions of nutrition, the more people I will be able to help.

I consider myself a personal trainer, motivator, life coach, nutrition consultant, educator, mentor, and leader. I know that's a lot, and I do not claim to know everything there is to know about these subjects. But I will give you a promise right now:

I will never stop learning how the body works!

I will never stop learning about nutrition!

Chapter 19 – Mission Statement: Purpose In Life

I will never stop learning about what motivates people!

I will never stop learning the best ways to achieve goals!

And, most important, Tonto and I also promise to share with you the best practices I learn about all these things to assure that you win the game of life!

Chapter 20 – Travel! See the World—It's Beautiful

Here I stand, on St. Pete Beach, Florida. I am visiting my brother Andy and his wife, Kim, and they live here year round. They are terrific hosts and are making my stay most enjoyable. I have never been to this place before; it is absolutely beautiful. I went for a run on the beach this morning, took a swim in the ocean, and visited the Don CeSar Hotel and got a little local history.

This world is huge, and there are so many beautiful places to see. I encourage everyone to go out and explore new places on the planet.

When I moved to Bremerhaven, Germany, in 1997, I recall the human resources manager saying to me, "*Nach dieser Reise, Sie sehen die Welt aus anderen Augen.*" Now, when he said that to me, I had no

Chapter 20 – Travel! See The World—It's Beautiful

friggin' idea what he was talking about. So he translated for me: "After your stay in Germany, you will look at the world with a different set of eyes."

That was absolutely true. When I returned to America after two years, I looked at the world differently. I had so much more appreciation for what we have here in the United States—all the things we take for granted. And I also appreciated the German culture, history, and their way of life.

Even after just four days here at St. Pete Beach, I will travel back to Boston tomorrow and again will look at the world a little differently. My time spent in this new part of the country where I have never been before has changed me.

I was so fortunate to live in Europe for two years. I traveled to a different location every two weeks. These are the places I visited:

Europe

Venice, Italy	Innsbruck, Austria	Prague, Czech Rep.
Paris, France	Amsterdam, Holland	Zürich, Switzerland
Brussels, Belgium	Strasbourg, France	Barcelona, Spain
Copenhagen, Denmark		

Germany

Munich, Berlin, Cologne, Bremen, Bremerhaven, Bamberg, Rüdesheim am Rhein, Rothenberg ob der Tauber, Heidelberg, and Koblenz

Other places I have visited or vacationed:

Cancun, Mexico   Puerto Rico   Montreal, Canada

Toronto, Canada   Vancouver Island, British Columbia

United States

New Orleans, Las Vegas and Washington D.C.

Chicago, Kansas City, Savanna, Atlanta, Dallas, Kennebunkport, and the beautiful White Mountains of New Hampshire

Florida

Fort Lauderdale, Miami, Orlando, Fort Myers, St. Pete Beach, Sanibel Island, and Captiva Island

Just writing down all these places gets me excited to see more! You don't have to go on expensive trips. I bet there are places within a three-hour drive from where you live that could be fun long-weekend trips.

At my house on the Cape hangs a picture on the wall. It reads:

Chapter 20 – Travel! See The World—it's Beautiful

My mom made this. I think it's needlepoint or cross-stitch or cross-fit—something like that.

I have been working very hard the past few months, basically working three jobs and writing this book. Yesterday, I took time to enjoy life's simple treasures.

I packed up my beach travel kit, which includes a radio, a cooler (filled with a twelve-pack of Coors Light and a large roast-beef sub), a towel, a beach chair, and suntan lotion, all loaded onto a neat, two-wheel device my brother gave to me. It has a pullout handle like a suitcase that can be wheeled through the airport. I walked down to the beach and spent six hours there, just chillaxing, watching the sights, swimming, and enjoying a beautiful summer day.

Many of us have busy lives, and there are only twenty-four hours in a day and 365 of those per year. We can't change that. We do control how we use each day. We don't want to work so hard that one day we wake up, look in the mirror, and say, "What the $%^&! Where did the time go?"

Because honestly, if we do not take time to enjoy life's simple treasures, this game of life is not that fun to play!

Work hard, play hard = Work efficiently, enjoy life!

Do you have a list of places you want to visit in your lifetime? If you don't, take just twenty minutes to sit down at your computer, because you are going to want to look up some of these places on the Internet to view pictures and read about them. Take a sheet of paper and start writing down the places you want to see.

This exercise will excite you and motivate you to achieve more so you can make these trips happen.

> The world is a book, and those who do not
> travel read only one page.
>
> —Saint Augustine

Chapter 21 – Mistakes and Decision-Making

The best definition of a mistake I have ever heard is: A mistake is successfully finding out what you never want to repeat. Everybody makes mistakes—some a lot bigger than others.

I am going to be fifty years old at the end of this year, and I would like to say, "That's it. I am not going to make any more mistakes. I have learned enough in life, and I will only make logical, smart decisions from now on!" It sounds pretty good, doesn't it? Is it realistic? Probably not! I will likely make a few more bubbleheaded decisions that my family and friends will laugh at. As long as I make someone laugh or smile, that's OK!

If I don't make any more mistakes in life, that probably means I didn't take enough risks, try enough new things, or challenge myself aggressively.

Here's an important point: mistakes are OK—if you learn from them! To make the same mistake more than once is an issue. To learn from other people's mistakes is smart!

I love the story about the smartass who asked Thomas Edison during an interview: "How does it feel to have failed making the light bulb nine thousand times?"

Thomas said to the young man, "You are looking at this all wrong. I have successfully found nine thousand ways not to make the light bulb! I don't believe anybody else on this planet can say that. Why should I quit now? Success is almost in my grasp." Not long after that interview, and after ten thousand total attempts, Thomas Edison invented the light bulb!

So, what are your biggest mistakes in life? Have you learned from them? What can we do differently moving forward that will prevent us from making mistakes and poor decisions?

- Think before we speak or react.

- Avoid too much alcohol.

- If our blood pressure is up and we are really irritated about something, we should take time to cool off, analyze the problem, and make the right decision.

If I look back on my biggest mistakes, those real estate moves I mentioned earlier jump out—not selling my Hyannis house at the peak of the market and investing in that land in Florida. But I took risks, and I learned from them. What I learned is that equity in a house can vanish overnight, so be careful when borrowing money from it. And land alone does not bring in any income.

Another mistake I made was not buying my parents' house or helping them keep the house when they couldn't afford it.

We grew up in a beautiful, big house right on the ocean in Nahant, Massachusetts. The house had five bedrooms, four bathrooms, and a fantastic layout, including a terrific sun porch and deck that overlooked the Boston skyline. We had a boat moored in front of the house.

My dad bought this house for $78,000 in 1975. Currently, that house is worth around $800,000.

Chapter 21 – Mistakes And Decision-making

My dad's business hit a few bad spots at times, and he borrowed off the equity in the house a few times. I obviously didn't learn from that—my mind was being used for chicks and beers at that time!

When it got to the point where he could not afford the house, the mortgage payment was around $3,000 per month, and he owed around $385,000. The market had dropped significantly at this time; I recall him getting an offer for the house for $305,000 in 1996, which was not enough to cover the amount he owed.

I had just accepted an overseas assignment with my company—a two-to-three-year management exchange program with a company in Germany. I was nervous and excited about this move. I had no idea what I was in for. I did not know what the cost of living would be. I had no clue whether I would have enough money to take over the payment of the Nahant house.

Honestly, something else that I thought of prior to my move was: if I bought the house, my parents would stay right where they were, and I would come back from Germany and live with them. Most people wouldn't want to still be living with their parents in their thirties.

As it turns out, I made great money over in Europe. I could have stayed at a less expensive apartment, driven a less expensive car, and taken over the payments on my parents' house.

My mom is up in heaven now, and my dad is in the nursing home, where I spend time with him each week. He has serious dementia, and it is very hard to communicate with him now. And to think, I could have spent much more time with them both in a beautiful house on the ocean!

Lesson to be learned for you kids out there: your parents won't be around forever. Cherish the times you can spend with them! Also, if they possess a nice home, land, or other investment that you want to keep in the family, give it some serious thought. And don't be afraid to discuss it with them! I wish I had!

I don't even call that a mistake, on my Dad's part. He was actually very smart with that house. He used the equity in the house to keep his business going long enough till all us kids had grown up, started our careers and moved out. It was just my Dad and Mom living there and the house was really too big and costly for the both of them. Also, If he had held onto the house all this time, it would have to be sold to pay for the cost of the nursing home he is currently in. I know a man who does exactly that, his Mom is in a nursing home and they had to sell her large house to pay for the costs. He writes a check to that nursing home for $10,000 each month. He told me how much he hates writing that check. My Dad's cost are covered my his pension plan, social security and the Mass Health plan. He would not of qualified for the Mass Health plan if he owned a $800,000 house.

A mistake is usually the result of a poor decision. We make hundreds of decisions each week. Some are small, like choosing what to order off a menu, which clothes to wear, and what to watch on TV. Others are much bigger: "What type of car should I purchase?" or "Which house should I buy?" Which college should you attend, or which job should you choose? Or how about this one: "Should I ask her to marry me?" These decisions have a much bigger impact on a person's life.

So how can we be assured we make the best choices on important decisions?

This is one method I use that I believe results in the best decisions. I allocate some time to make the decision, usually two hours during my peak-performance time when my mind is working very efficiently. With me, this time is around 9:00 a.m., after I have had a good breakfast and

Chapter 21 – Mistakes And Decision-making

I am sitting at my dining room table with a nice cup of coffee. If I had a great night's sleep and ate well, had no alcohol, and worked out hard the day before, then my mind operates most effectively. Then I write out the pros and cons of each decision.

I want to share with you a real-life, real-time, important decision I am making this week.

The tenant at my Hyannis property just sent me an e-mail giving me his notice. He will be moving out at the end of next month. It is the first week in August, and he will be moving out September 30. He has been an excellent tenant for the past five years, and I have owned the house for ten years.

So, here is the decision I need to make:

Option 1—Get another tenant to move in October 1.

Option 2—Sell my three-bedroom house in Hyannis.

This is a pretty big decision because what I decide is going to affect my life for at least the next few years, perhaps longer. It is also one of those decisions where, if I make the wrong choice, I could regret it for a long time.

Say I decide to sell the house, and the housing market in Hyannis starts to increase steadily over the next five years. I can envision sitting around with my family or friends and them saying to me, "Wow, Tom. You bonehead. You should have held on to that house; you could have gotten an extra hundred thousand dollars if you sold it today!"

Or if I don't sell, I could rent it to someone who turns out to be a nightmare of a tenant. I may have trouble collecting the rent, or he or she might not keep the place clean. Then major house-maintenance issues would come up, like the need for a new furnace or roof. Now I envision sitting around with those same folks, and they are saying, "Wow, Tom. You bonehead. You should have gotten rid of that house when you had the chance. You wouldn't have all these headaches now!"

I don't care so much about what other people say, but I would be saying the exact same thing.

OK, so now I should make the right decision! Let me share with you this decision-making process. It is funny: Tonto jumped up on my shoulder and quickly said, "Get rid of it. Get some cash for it and reduce your headaches." Sometimes, this is called a gut instinct.

Let me share with you some facts:

> The current mortgage payment on the house is $1,199.
>
> The rent I have been receiving is $1,200.
>
> The amount I owe on the house is $137,600.

With many decisions, research is needed to help with your decision, and you will want to call certain people to get their opinions. I recommend, however, that you contact the experts for their opinion *after* you go through this exercise so you have more information and can respond more intelligently to their questions.

Let me share with you some of the results of my research:

The average rental amount people are paying for a three-bedroom house in Hyannis is $1,400 per month. I called my real estate friend to

Chapter 21 – Mistakes And Decision-making

verify that number, and she said that $1,300 per month is more realistic for my property.

The average home sale on three-bedroom houses in Hyannis is around $189,800. Say I listed it at $199,000 and ended up agreeing on a $192,000 price. $9,600 would go to the real estate agent and $4,000 to the lawyer and closing costs. That leaves me with $41,187 going into my pocket.

The following chart shows some relative data:

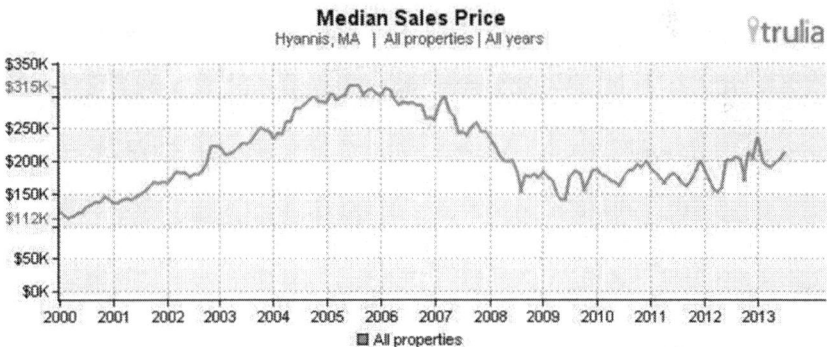

A couple things just jump out from this chart. Yes, the time to sell was 2005. Look at that drop: from $315,000 to $150,000 in four years. The line has been steadily increasing, but painfully slowly. If God would just send me the chart for ten years from now today, that would be awesome—it would help with my decision! I guess that would be too easy—no fun in that.

Let me throw in another curve ball to spice things up a little. My tenant who is moving out sent me another e-mail a few days ago. He has a good friend that is interested in taking over the lease if I decide not to sell. I actually stopped by the house this past weekend to assess any work needed, and I met this other young man. It appears that he would make a great tenant. He works for a landscaper and would take care of the lawn, trash removal, and snow removal at no cost to me. I also told him I would have to go up $100 in the rent, and he had no problem with that.

Some of you, in your own mind, have made a decision, correct?

OK, let's do our analysis exercise. I am sitting down at my dining room table with a nice cup of joe.

Side thought: Where did the term cup of joe *come from? Here is what I found on coffeefaq.com: The US Navy used to serve alcoholic beverages onboard ships. But when Admiral Josephus "Joe" Daniels became Chief of Naval Operations, he outlawed alcohol onboard ships except for very special occasions. Coffee then became the beverage of choice; hence the term* cup of joe.

We have four categories of pros and cons for each decision, and we are going to spend twenty minutes on each category, using a timer, to list all the things that come to mind for it. Do not spend seventy minutes on one and fifteen minutes on another because you are leaning that way.

The four categories are as follows:

1. Renting: Pros

2. Renting: Cons

3. Selling: Pros

4. Selling: Cons

OK, here we go. Start the timer.

Chapter 21 – Mistakes And Decision-making

#1—Renting Pros

- o I could potentially earn more money selling the house a few years from now.

- o I could hold on to it long enough to make enough money from that sale to pay off my other Cape Cod property, which is one of my long-term goals.

- o I have a tenant lined up, and he appears be a good fit.

- o The tenant does landscaping and knows how to address most building maintenance issues.

- o It's nice to say to people that I have two houses at the Cape; it provides leverage in some cases.

- o The house is closer to Main Street than my other house.

- o It could be the summer retirement home at the Cape that costs a lot less. I could pay it off quicker, maintenance costs are lower, taxes are lower, and insurance is less.

- o It could be a revenue stream down the road. The house would be all paid for and I could have $1,500 per month coming in to supplement my income.

- o The house has some memories with my family and has some sentimental value, which will be a little sad to let go of.

- o Being a rental property, all work done on it and associated costs are tax deductible.

#2—Renting Cons

- You are a landlord twenty-four hours a day and need to address any issues that come up.

- The rent check is not guaranteed every month and could be an issue down the road.

- Currently, I am just getting by financially. Any major maintenance problems will present a financial problem, and the house is due for them. I have been pretty lucky the past few years and have had no big maintenance issues, which could mean some are coming.

- One of my longer-term goals is to have just one mortgage payment on my Isalene house, sell this one and my Danvers property, and relocate to the Fort Lauderdale area. So why not sell it now?

- Being a landlord does create some stress throughout the year.

- Time is essential, and holding on to this piece of property will undoubtedly consume some time each month. Whether it is paying the bills, addressing maintenance issues, or dealing with tenant issues, I would rather spend that time doing things that are much more pleasurable.

- I am tired of being a landlord.

Chapter 21 – Mistakes And Decision-making

- I am tired of working on all these house projects.

- It's not like I don't have enough energy to deal with these things. I have plenty of energy. I would just prefer to use it in other areas, like learning, traveling, working out, hiking, biking, and fishing.

- We only go around this game of life once; do I want to spend a portion of it being a landlord?

- The furnace on the house is very old and could go any year now.

- The neighborhood is not the best in the area. The house got broken into once, and that could result in lower home value down the road or rental turnover.

- I have been very lucky with an excellent tenant for the past five years; I should count my blessings and get out while I can.

- This new tenant would have various friends staying over at the house, and some partying would be going on.

#3—Selling Pros

o This will put money in my pocket—actually, in my savings account—probably between $30,000 and $40,000.

o I have been financially strapped for the last nine years, and I have had to reduce my spending in many areas, depriving me of some of the finer things in life. I could get some of those back now.

o It would free up time to do things I really enjoy doing.

o I would have fewer headaches and less stress from the rental property.

o Additional money in my bank account and freed-up time will help my social life. I can go on dates without feeling guilty for spending too much money or thinking I really should be working on that home improvement project right now.

o It is more in line with my goal to relocate back to Florida.

o There is a lot of work that needs to be done in the process of selling that house, like getting rid of all the furniture and accumulated junk. Also getting the house ready for the market, like painting and cleaning. It will be nice to put all that work behind me.

o Currently the house is in pretty good shape. A few years from now, it might need much more work to get it ready for the market.

o More money in my bank account now helps me purchase better gifts for my nieces, nephews, and other family members at Christmas, birthdays, graduations, and special events. I have not done a great job at that over the past eight years.

Chapter 21 – Mistakes And Decision-making

- Freed-up time also allows me to attend special events and spend more time with family and friends.

- I will have money to make some needed improvements on my Isalene property, which will increase its rental value and bring in more income there.

- It will also make the Isalene property a better vacation spot for my family and friends by adding bikes, kayaks, and improved living space.

- I get excited at the thought of unloading this property and getting into a better financial situation.

- I would much rather spend my time doing things like I am doing now—writing a book or making an exercise video, producing an audio version of this book, and designing my own fitness facility—than spend it being a landlord and addressing house-maintenance issues.

- I have a good real estate agent and real estate attorney that I trust, and they both work very well together, which should make the process smooth. That team might not be available in the future.

- I have had to borrow money out of my 401k during some of the past years because money was so tight. Selling would significantly reduce the chance of needing to do that again.

- I can learn the process of selling so that I can eventually sell my Danvers property on my own.

#4—Selling Cons

- It might not be the best time to sell. The market appears to be lagging behind the Boston North Shore area, maybe even by two to five years.

- Statistics show that real estate always pays off in the long term and that holding on to this property probably is the best financial move.

- This house could provide a place where one or more of my family members or friends could live if they run into trouble down the road.

- Selling would create a lot of work right now: getting the house ready for the market by cleaning and painting, selling furniture, and getting rid of junk.

- I could keep it and hire a property management company to deal with all the tenant and maintenance issues.

- The house was worth $300,000 at the height of the market in 2005. If I sell now, I will always think about the money I could have made and that I didn't hold on to the property long enough to get back to that point.

OK, my time ran out. I spent twenty minutes on each category.

While doing this exercise, you might think right away that the pros of one category match the cons of another. And, in fact, they

Chapter 21 – Mistakes And Decision-making

usually do. However, asking the question both ways usually results in a few extra bullet points somewhere, which could be a deciding factor.

For the mathematical summary, you add up the pros of renting (#1) and the cons of selling (#4) and compare it to the cons of renting (#2) and the pros of selling (#3).

And the score is sixteen to thirty-one in favor of selling the house. The answer is quite clear. I feel good with this analysis, and the house will go up for sale.

When you do this type of analysis, usually one jumps out at you and becomes obvious. If the only objective was to make the most money out of this real estate investment, I could see the answer going the other way. However, I believe it is more about quality of life and time spent with family and friends. Money is important, but to focus only on money and to lose sight of the things money cannot buy is foolish.

I used this analysis when I made my career change, and it was quite clear what I needed to do.

Try this approach when you need to make an important decision. I am going to bet that 90 percent of the time, the answer will be clear, and you will feel good about your decision.

If you are still uncertain after this exercise, then it is time to seek educated and experienced opinions from others—but you will be much better prepared to receive their input. A lot of times, people ask for advice from folks who have no knowledge or experience on the topic.

Use your brain first; it is an incredible tool that only you possess!

THOMAS EDWARD MUSER

When you find your path, you must not be afraid. You need to have sufficient courage to make mistakes. Disappointment, defeat, and despair are the tools God uses to show us the way.

—Paulo Coelho (from *Brida*)

Chapter 22 – The Value and Importance of Time

Has someone ever said to you, "I would love to, but I just don't have the time?" You always hear comments like this: "I would love to work out every day; I just don't have the time." Or, "I wish I had the time to prepare my food the night before; I could save money and eat healthier." I could go on and on, but actually, I don't think that would be an effective use of time.

Everybody has been given the same amount of time each day. This makes the game of life fair. If some people were given thirty hours per day and other people only fourteen, the people with thirty hours would have a significant advantage toward succeeding in life if they used their time wisely.

Everybody gets twenty-four hours per day. That adds up to 1,440 minutes each day. How a person utilizes those minutes determine who he or she becomes. It is so important not to waste any of those minutes; you can never get them back. Once the day is over, the way those 1,440 minutes were used can never be changed.

When people say to you that they don't have the time, they are really lying. They have the time: 1,440 minutes per day. If they were honest, they should be saying, "I would rather use my minutes doing something else." It is all about making priorities.

> A man who dares to waste one hour of life has not discovered the value of life.
>
> —Charles Darwin

If someone asked you to do something and you knew it would not be an effective use of your time, you could say, "I am sorry, but I have already committed that time toward completing some tasks that will help me achieve a very important goal I have set for myself." In short, "I'm very sorry, but I have some other tasks that I need to get done today. Thanks for understanding!"

How do you know if you are using your minutes effectively? That's easy. You just ask yourself, "Is what I am doing going to help me achieve the goals I set for myself? Or does this task have absolutely nothing to do with the goals I have set for myself?"

You may be saying, "Hey, these minutes seem pretty important. Any way I can get some more of these things?" Yes; I believe that using some of your minutes each day toward exercise, eating right, and getting enough sleep can add minutes to the end of your life—perhaps years! Also, by spending a few minutes planning your day, you end up working more efficiently and that frees up some minutes during the day.

Has someone ever said to you, "I'm just killing time"? That freaks me out—"killing" time. If you don't want your minutes of life, give them to me!

It probably has something to do with me turning fifty this year. It is quite clear to me now that we don't live forever. Recently, I have attended wakes and funerals for people not much older than me, and some younger, who are now all done with their minutes.

Chapter 22 – The Value And Importance Of Time

When you are in your twenties and thirties, you don't think about these minutes at all. I believe your mind is too busy thinking about other things, like "Which club or party should I go to this weekend?" or school events and stuff like that.

Now I want to use my minutes as efficiently as possible. I do not want to waste one minute if I can help it. For example, there is so much I want to get done today, it exceeds mathematically the time available: my 1,440 minutes. As Brian Tracy says, you will never get caught up! The only way to free up some of your time is to stop doing certain tasks that are of low priority and/or not related to your goals.

Other examples where we are spending our minutes include mowing lawns, doing landscaping, cleaning and maintaining homes or properties—these are very time-consuming. I know it saves us some money to do these things ourselves, and right now, financially it might make sense. But to create more time, to achieve other goals we have set for ourselves, we might have to hire someone to do some or all of those tasks.

How do we know which items to outsource and which ones to do ourselves?

I have always been a little paranoid about hiring other people for this work. I thought they would not be able to do the job as well I would. I could save the money and do it myself. Lately, though, the last two contractors I hired to do work on my properties exceeded my expectations, and that's a beautiful thing. I realized this was a very smart move. They performed the work better than I would have, and I got to utilize the time for something more valuable.

Working out is a great example. I can put someone through a twenty-five-minute workout that burns more calories and is more beneficial than what 75 percent of the people who come to the gym do for an hour or more. I see it every day!

Working Out versus Time

When I was in my thirties, I used to think that if I did not have an hour to work out, I should blow it off because it wouldn't be effective.

What a knucklehead I was! Today, I sneak in a fourteen-minute workout whenever I can. I don't care if is seven minutes, sixteen minutes, or twenty-three minutes. Get it in! They add up over the years!

Let me give you an example of a quick workout:

Yesterday, I had a very busy day. I trained a bunch of people and was about to head out to my bartending job. I was going to leave the gym without working out, and then Tonto showed up. He told me to go get a quick, efficient workout. I went back and did TRX rows and TRX chest presses (three sets of each exercise), total gym (body-weight resistance) pull-ups, and total gym shoulder presses (three sets of each).

What an effective use of time—twelve sets in fourteen minutes!

Switching Gears

Have you ever described someone you know as "never getting out of second gear"?

We used to make fun of my good friend Mike as never getting beyond *third* gear. We worked together for over ten years, bartending at the Porthole Pub in Lynn. As a bartender, you need to switch gears to match the customer flow. Some are very good at it, and some are not.

We switch gears when we need to; it's that simple. Let me give you an example:

Chapter 22 – The Value And Importance Of Time

You set your alarm clock for 7:00 a.m. because you have an important meeting at 9:00 a.m. But your alarm clock does not go off! You wake up at 8:15. You freak out, get washed up, get a quick bite to eat, and make the appointment at 9:00 a.m. You were in sixth gear during that period of time.

Why don't we operate in sixth gear all the time?

Because it is not easy! We silly humans choose the path of least resistance most of the time!

Now, I believe it is good to kick back and enjoy life whenever possible. Though that is absolutely true, I also believe we need to work in fifth and sixth gear. It will yield you the financial rewards that will optimize your happiness on this planet!

I am a little behind my game plan for writing this book right now. Why am I behind? Well, I have priorities—some other tasks to complete before I sit down and write. Some of these tasks fall under my current goals. But some tasks that I have chosen to do instead of writing do not. Those tasks provide some instant gratification, like watching an NFL football game, a movie, or a silly TV program. The TV can kill your productivity.

If someone came up to me and said, "If you finish your book by the end of the month, I will give you one million dollars cash." It is the first week in September; I would have three and a half weeks to complete it. You know what? I would finish it!

For example, on the last day before your vacation, you take care of everything you need to get done on that last day. You are operating in sixth gear, at peak efficiency.

This past weekend, I had planned on bringing my laptop down to Starbucks, getting a triple espresso, and writing ten pages in my book. Then I would reward myself and get a couple of beers at the Sylvan Street Grill.

Instead, I was hungry around 6:00 p.m. after I mowed the lawn. I had been craving Chinese food all week long. *I decided* to walk down to the Hong Kong Café for some food. After a plate of beef lo mein and two mai tais, *I decided* to walk across the street to the Maple Street Tavern. After drinking three Brooklyn lagers and listening to some live music, *I decided* to walk home. At home, *I decided* to pop in a movie and have a few more beers. The ten pages never got written.

It does bring us back to self-discipline (the ability to make yourself do what you should do, when you should do it, whether you feel like it or not). You can see in the above paragraph the italicized words *I decided*. I chose instant gratification over long-term completion of an important goal.

How did I feel the next day? Terrible. I did not complete the task I had planned for the day, and I was a little hungover to boot.

Make your minutes count; you can never get them back once the day's over!

The Difference between Living and Existing

After my mom went up to heaven, I found myself spending more time in church. I would attend Mass on Sunday and hang out in the church after the Mass had ended and just reflect on life and think about my mom.

I was walking out of the church one day and ran into the priest. His name is Father Daniel, and we started talking. I shared with him

Chapter 22 – The Value And Importance Of Time

my mom's battle with cancer and the last few months of her life. He introduced me to these words: *living* and *existing*. He explained that, with today's medical advances, doctors, hospitals, and nursing homes can keep people alive for years. Many of these people are existing, but they are not living.

Unfortunately, I see this every week when I visit my dad in the nursing home. His roommate is in awful shape; he can't move, he has four hours of dialysis each day, and he has a tumor growing out of his head. He is existing but not living.

It is really sad to see! So why do I share this depressing stuff with you? That's not me; I'm always positive and upbeat and look for the best in every situation. Yeah, that's me! I guess it is good once in a while, though, to make sure you are living and not just existing.

Get the most out of life! And remember, it does come to an end, so don't waste one minute!

> *Don't be fooled by the calendar. There are only as many days in the year as you make use of. One man gets only a week's value out of a year while another man gets a full year's value out of a week.*
>
> —Charles Richards

Chapter 23 – What Makes a Great Personal Trainer?

I share my thoughts on being a great personal trainer with you because it is my profession and currently my main purpose in life. I want to make sure you have all the information you need in case you are looking for a personal trainer or want to become one. I have had the opportunity and pleasure to hire, train, and work with hundreds of personal trainers. The ones that excel in this field have some outstanding qualities. Here are the qualities that I feel make them the best in the business:

1. They display a high-energy, positive attitude 100 percent of the time. Not four out of five days. 100 percent of the time. You see this clearly the first time you meet them. You can feel their energy and enthusiasm. You can even feel their energy over the phone. This was one of the nicest compliments I have ever received: the person said to me, "I could feel your energy just from the voice mail you left me." These trainers smile, and you can tell they really enjoy their profession. They leave any problems or issues they have in their personal lives at home. They know how to control their emotions and stay focused on the client's goals 100 percent of the time.

2. They have the knowledge it takes to get the results the client wants in a safe and effective program. Experience and continuing education is key! They should have the desire to continually improve their

Chapter 23 – What Makes A Great Personal Trainer?

education in the fitness and nutrition field. So a great question to ask them is, in addition to their current degrees and/or certifications, what is the next certification or educational class they plan on taking?

A degree in exercise science, exercise physiology, or kinesiology is fantastic. A certification in personal training and CPR/AED is a must. Unfortunately, there are too many personal training certifications in the field—probably around one hundred—and the top 10 percent clearly outweigh the others in quality. Five of the most well-respected and recognized PT certifications are NSCA-CSCS, NSCA-CPT, ACSM-CPT, NASM-CPT and ACE-CPT. There are other good ones out there; you can research them online to check them out. One quick way to tell if a certification is good is to look at the cost. The good ones usually run between $500 and $1000. If you see any for $99, ignore them.

Be careful, though, that you don't use education as your only criterion for hiring or being a personal trainer. I have been burned by doing that a few times. I hired people because they were very book smart and could answer all the anatomy questions I threw at them. Within a few months, they failed, usually because they didn't know how to talk to people.

3. They are punctual; they start the session on time and end it on time. They are never late for an appointment. I have taken over personal trainer teams, and unfortunately, I found that some of

their trainers had these bad habits. I recall noticing one person who was starting her sessions late and then ending them late, running over into the next session. When I asked her about this, the reply was, "Oh, it's OK. All my clients know that if I start late, we will end late, and the next client will understand." In her mind, this seemed to make it right. But when I talked with her clients, I knew it was not. That trainer did not last long. Another trainer was always running in the door while still getting dressed—putting his shirt on and arriving for the session three minutes late. The best in the business are ready ten minutes before, preparing and working on the clients' programs when they arrive. With back-to-back clients, they end one minute early and start the next session on time.

4. They know how to manage their schedules. They work the hours they plan on working and do not deviate from their desired work schedule. They do not try to move their clients from here to there just to accommodate their personal lives. They never cancel an appointment. They are accommodating and understanding for their clients when emergencies and difficult situations arise. I have seen many new personal trainers make the mistake of planning training sessions whenever they can get them. It's an easy mistake to make; they are trying to build a business and they need clients. They come in early, stay late, work weekends—whatever it takes to do more sessions. What happens, though, is that it's not sustainable, and something else always suffers, like sleep, family, nutrition, and other important tasks.

Chapter 23 – What Makes A Great Personal Trainer?

Good trainers also make clear the rules of cancelling an appointment. Most use a twenty-four-hour policy. If clients cancel within twenty-four hours of the appointment, they are charged for it. The logic here is that twenty-four hours provides enough time for the personal trainer to put someone else in that slot so he or she can get paid for it. I made this mistake at first; I was too nice and wouldn't charge for late cancellations. Then I realized that it was really affecting my paycheck, and I needed to put food on the table. Also, it is better for the client, if they know they are going to be charged for it, chances are they will make it in, keeping their fitness program on track.

5. They know how to deliver that first, most important session—you know, that complimentary session most gyms give you when you join. I have heard this session called many things: fitness evaluation, fitness consultation, personal fitness workout, starter session, and free personal training session. No matter what it is called, here is what it should contain:

    a. Proper scheduling of the event.

    b. An energetic, friendly greeting.

    c. An exchange of contact information.

    d. A review of health history.

    e. A review of previous strength training and cardiovascular activities.

    f. Most important: finding out what the new member wants to get out of the fitness program.

    g. Now enough information is known to do the proper assessments. Great personal trainers know how to do all the necessary assessments: blood pressure, circumference measurements, body composition, endurance testing, balance, and strength—upper body, core, lower body, and squat—assessment.

    h. Time permitting, they will show you a few exercises based on your fitness goals.

    i. Wrap up—they give the client a professional opinion on the best options to achieve the results he or she wants.

Just a side note on this complimentary session: hundreds of people each day throughout the country turn down this complimentary session because they believe they know enough. A huge mistake! Even with my fitness education and experience, if I moved to California, joined a gym, and they offered me this session, I would jump on it in a heartbeat. I would ask for a personal trainer with good experience and education and who has been with the gym for at least one year. Why would you pass up the opportunity to speak with a fitness professional about *your* fitness program and *your* health? Of course, the trainer will try to sell you personal training; that is the profession. If the trainer has not presented a good case and plan for you to achieve your fitness goals, you just say no.

Chapter 23 – What Makes A Great Personal Trainer?

6. The best personal trainers know how to present the best options that fit within their clients' budgets and will get them the results they desire. I have seen a bunch of new personal trainers not make it in the business because they did not know how to present the best options and ask for the money.

7. They know how to work the fitness floor. When personal trainers go out onto the fitness floor, they are on stage. Most of them do not realize this, but everyone is watching them: the members, the employees, and even the other personal trainers. They greet and are courteous with other members but don't strike up conversations with them during the client's time. They know how to work with other members and trainers with regard to sharing equipment and space. They know how to adapt and change a planned routine on the fly if the equipment or space becomes unavailable. They are serious and professional while smiling and having fun.

8. They are focused on results! They have a clear understanding of exactly what the client's goals are. They know how to design the most effective program for the client. They reevaluate or do periodic assessments on key areas to make sure the client is on track for achieving goals. They make adjustments and changes when necessary. They keep the workouts effective, fun, and challenging. They know how to push a client far enough to get results in a safe manner without injuries.

9. Last, but not least, a great personal trainer knows *it's all about the clients*. It is their money; it is their time! Great personal trainers don't spend the majority of the session talking about themselves. They adapt to meet the requests of the client, and if those requests will not get the desired results, they are up front and explain why things need to be done a certain way.

The most rewarding part of my job as a personal trainer is when clients come in and they can't wait to share their latest heath improvements with me. I can tell before they say anything by the bounce in their steps and the smiles on their faces. They will say things like, "I dropped three pant sizes," or "My doctor took me off blood pressure medicine," or "My daughter noticed my toned arms."

One client came in one day smiling and told me how she carried her laundry basket down the flight of stairs to the basement. Prior to that she set it at the top of the stairs and kicked it down the stairs. It would hit the bottom and the clothes would fly all over. She had lost seventy pounds and being able to carry that basket down the stairs was a nice accomplishment. The same person was putting out the spring outdoor furniture, carrying tables and chairs with ease, her kids looked at her in amazement and said, "Wow mom how did you get so strong?"

Another client of mine, a doctor of around sixty years of age, who got tremendous results in strength and changing his body composition was out mowing his lawn in a tank top. A car pulled over and two of the nurses he works with got out and walked over to him. They said, "oh my God, we never knew how buff and muscular you are!" I think he really enjoyed telling me that story.

Chapter 23 – What Makes A Great Personal Trainer?

Another client came back from her family reunion in another part of the country and shared with me some of the reactions her family commented on. Some of these family members haven't seen her in years and were amazed at the shape she was in. She changed her body composition from 30% body fat to 14%. One of her relatives said, "what did you do, leave the other half of your self in Boston?"

That is what makes it all worthwhile, that is why I do what I do!

Chapter 24 – The Game of Life

I often think about life as a game we play. Some days we win, and some days we lose. I can recall walking out of the food-processing plant at the end of my shift when I was working as a production supervisor and Tonto saying, "Wow, Tom, you got your ass kicked today." I lost that day.

The goal is to win more days than you lose. Fortunately, I am winning more days than losing now, and I attribute that to following the techniques I outlined in the first four chapters of this book. I cannot honestly say what it's like to win the game of life, because I am still playing. I believe everyone should play the game of life as if they will live to be one hundred. I plan on living till I am a hundred. Why not plan for that? Should I plan to live to sixty-two? Heck, no! I am forty-nine years old right now, and when I hit fifty at the end of the year, I will be halfway through the game. I like to compare it to a football game. So when I reach fifty, it's half time. If I had to give myself a score for the first half, I would be winning twenty-one to thirteen. It's still a close game. If I screw up, I could lose this game.

What's the score of your game? Are you winning or losing? If you're around twenty-five years old, you've made it through the first quarter, and if you're seventy-five, you've completed three quarters.

What do they do at half time? Well, they do have a huge half time celebration at the Super Bowl. Celebrating is a great idea! The other thing teams and players do at half time is make adjustments to their game plan. They analyze what's working well and what isn't working.

Chapter 24 – The Game Of Life

I believe we should do the same. A great exercise to do is to take out two sheets of paper; on the top of one, you write, "What's working well," and at the top of the other, you write, "What's not working." Then, with that nice cup of joe, write down all the things that come to mind on both, take 20 minutes on both. This usually ends up producing more goals and tasks that will help you win the game.

Like with every game, there are rules. In the game of life, most are called "laws." We do not want to do anything illegal or be dishonest. We want to win the game with integrity, honesty, hard work, and good values!

My aunt Marion lived till she was 104; I believe she won the game of life. She was always so happy and positive. I would have to say her positive high energy fun attitude is what got her to 104. When our family went to visit her, she was the best host, always feeding us and providing us kids with games and fun activities.

When I am no longer breathing, it would be nice for people to say, "Tom won the game of life!" But, most important, I want to help as many people as possible also win the game of life. It would be great going to my final resting place knowing that I have helped many people live a more rewarding, fulfilling, and successful life.

In my game, I am really looking forward to the second half. I know that if I learn from the mistakes I made and put my best effort forward, utilizing all the skills and talents the Good Lord gave me, I will win the game by a large margin. Now, I can tell, you are starting to get excited about playing your game. You have already started thinking about changes you are going to make, and you've identified the skills and talents you possess. No doubt about it, the game of life is fun and exciting.

I almost made a mistake last month but caught myself. My brother Dan and I went to look at log cabins. I made an appointment with the salesperson and told her what we were looking for. We met with her, picked out the log cabin kit that we thought would be best for our family, and she gave us the price: $40,000. Between six kids, that could be a good investment.

Then I remembered my Cape houses that were also bought at good prices. I did not consider all the additional expenses that come with owning houses. I did not calculate the utilities, maintenance, repairs, tax increases, and the *time* it takes to deal with all these things. You don't get that time back! You could spend that time doing things that earn real money or bring you great joy!

What woke me up was the DVD the saleswoman gave me on how to construct this log cabin. I still think that if my brothers, sister, and I took one month off from work and built this log cabin, it would be a terrific, fun, family-bonding experience with a lot of laughs, most of them about my brother Chris. I mean that in a good way, Chris makes himself an easy target for jokes. Truthfully I am very proud of him, he is an incredible Dad.

Toward the end of the DVD, it showed the man staining the log cabin. I hate painting, and this painting looked like a yearly event. That got me thinking of all the other time-consuming maintenance activities there would be, and these all cost money. Then I got to thinking about what I have heard about log cabins. Take the price of the kit and multiply it by three: that is what it will end up costing you. Then I thought about the taxes. Right now, we pay only on the land. Once the house gets built, the taxes will go up quite a bit.

So I asked myself, realistically, how often will I use it? I have a good friend that paid a lot of money for a big sailboat; he was so excited when he bought it. A year later, I asked him how the boat was. He said, "I have only used it four times." He sold it two years later for half the money he paid for it—probably not the best move.

Chapter 24 – The Game Of Life

Let me share this with you; this is good stuff: I had a boat for about fifteen years. I had an incredible amount of fun on it for the first ten. Then some things changed, like my job and where I was living, that made it difficult to have a lot of fun with the boat. I'll cut to the conclusion. I want to buy a boat again; however, I need three things before I do:

1. Time to use it (for example, if I work a four-day week and have every Friday, Saturday, and Sunday off)

2. Easy access to it (I live in a condo on the Intracoastal Waterway in Fort Lauderdale with a boat slip)

3. Money to put into it (I have additional funds coming in monthly that cover all associated costs)

Now, these three things could also apply to a lot of different situations, like the log cabin I was talking about. We want to get that log cabin built, however, we need those things like time to use it and money to put into it to make it really worthwhile. So ask yourself these questions before you make a big decision or investment. Do your homework with the associated costs; talk to people who have already made the same move. The Internet is fantastic for researching data.

When I was a kid, I came home from the sporting-goods store with a new hockey stick. I couldn't wait to show my dad. I said, "Hey, Dad, look at this great hockey stick I bought! It was such a good price."

He said, "It's only a good value if you're going to use it."

I don't recall using the hockey stick; I ended up playing football, basketball, and baseball, but no hockey. He was right; it was only a great investment if I used it all the time. That is important to think about when making any investment. How often are you going to use it?

This game of life should not be complicated, stressful, hectic, or chaotic. It should be fun, rewarding, challenging, and exciting.

We need to just swap these things around and change the words:

Complicated…to…simplified.

Stressful…to…peaceful and relaxing.

Hectic…to…in control.

Chaotic…to…efficient.

So you need to take a time-out occasionally and ask yourself: "What in my life is creating stress or making things complicated?" And reduce or eliminate these things.

Also, what in your life gives you the most pleasure and fun? What excites you when you think about it? What is most rewarding to you? Try to put more of these things into your life.

Not having enough money to pay the bills is probably one of the most common situations that cause stress in people's lives.

Unhappy relationships are probably right up there too.

Stressful, demanding jobs where people are working seventy to eighty hours a week, always on call, and bringing work home with them is something else I often see.

Chapter 24 – The Game Of Life

I have done personal training sessions where people need to vent for about fifteen minutes about things that are aggravating them about their jobs. Then they look at me and say, "I'm sorry, just had to get that off my chest. I'm feeling better already." By the end of the workout, they do feel better. I have said it many times: exercise is the best stress-relief medicine on the planet.

Dreading to go to work is something that we should all try to avoid. Looking forward to going into work is something we should all strive for!

It is never too late to start. If you are badly losing your game, thirty-seven to ten, you are thinking, "This game is over; I can't win this game." Wrong! Some of the best games in history were won with fantastic comebacks in the fourth quarter.

Let's make some bold moves and finish this game the right way!

Winning isn't everything—but wanting to win is.

—Vince Lombardi

Chapter 25 – Summary

All right, let's simplify this and make it easy to get started! I've summarized this book in seven paragraphs:

Tonto's Game Plan to Win

1. *Follow the three simple rules.* Make sure you are getting enough sleep (seven to eight hours). Make sure you are eating four to six well-balanced, nutritious meals per day. Make sure you are doing some type of workout six days per week, take one day off to rest! Each workout can be a combination of strength training and cardiovascular work or 3 days of strength and 3 days of cardio. Remember, something is better then nothing, a thirty-minute walk or a bike ride counts as cardio, a total-body conditioning class at your local gym counts as strength training.

    Do not go beyond this point if you don't have the items above under control!

2. *Set your goals for the year, with completion dates.* I suggest between eight to twelve goals. List the goals in the order of their importance to you and your family. Rewrite your goals every morning. At a minimum, reread your goals each morning. Remember, your goals should excite you and make

Chapter 25 — Summary

you feel good when you think about them. So, rewriting your goals each morning can give you an energetic and fantastic attitude all day long.

3. *Plan your day in advance.* You can do it the night before or first thing in the morning after a great breakfast with the mind well rested. Make a list of the tasks that you need to accomplish that day. These should be listed in the order they will be completed. Make sure your daily tasks match your goals! If there is a task on your list that is unrelated to your goals, think twice about doing it. It should take you around ten minutes each morning to rewrite your goals and write your daily tasks. This will be one of the most valuable uses of ten minutes you can have! Seriously, think about it. How often we waste ten minutes per day doing something totally worthless, maybe even harmful and unrelated to our desired goals!

4. *Become a master at self-discipline.* You need to discipline yourself to accomplish the daily tasks that are all related to your goals. This is easier said than done; the day will introduce many options for you to use your time differently. Most will be friends, family, and colleagues asking you to do something different from the tasks you put together. Some of these options will give you immediate satisfaction and pleasure; however, you must realize that they might pull you away from achieving your goals. The ability to hold yourself accountable and accomplish the daily tasks you put together, regardless of the temptations and offers you receive, will be a reward in itself and provide you with happiness.

5. *Have a positive, energetic, excited attitude 100 percent of the time,* This is also easier said than done; however, you are absolutely in control of your attitude! With practice, this will become one of the most important habits that will move you in the direction of accomplishing all your goals. Yesterday, I walked into the gym (my workplace) and greeted the three people at the front desk. When one of them asked, "How are you?" I replied, "Ridiculously fantastic!" One of them followed me into the break room, where I put my lunch away. And she said to me, "I want whatever you are smoking!" I set my attitude for that day, and so can you!

6. *Live your life with integrity, faith, hard work, and good, honest, solid values.* If you practice strong moral principles, they will become a habit, and you will be a role model for others. By doing the right thing, the honest thing in all situations, you'll display actions that are contagious and can breed a better place to live and work for everyone! Sometimes making the honest, right decision can create an uncomfortable situation for a short time; however, it always creates the best situation for the long term. You can ruin a successful life with just one dishonest action that you can never take back. To be known as an honest person with high integrity is one of the best compliments a person can receive! Believe in yourself, you are a talented unique special individual like no other and you have the ability to accomplish some fantastic achievements.

Chapter 25 – Summary

7. Enjoy life's simple treasures, and have fun! Remember, some of your daily tasks can be exciting, fun things that you love to do, like going to the beach, fishing, watching a great NFL game, and going to your favorite restaurant or vacation spot. I spent last Saturday hiking up in the White Mountains, New Hampshire, with my brothers and nephew. This was on my tasks list. It was a blast and is related to my goals about maintaining and improving family relations. And it was a workout, which is also on my goals list. The memories it created, watching my brother pinball down the mountain, are priceless and will be talked about for many years. These types of tasks and events are essential for a happy, successful life. To laugh and enjoy this planet makes it all worthwhile!

Brief **Version of Tonto's Game Plan to Win**

1. Follow the three simple rules—sleep 7 to 8 hours per day, eat right every day, and work out six days per week, take one day off.

2. Set your goals for the year, with completion dates.

3. Plan your day in advance with tasks related to your goals.

4. Become a master at self-discipline to assure completion of tasks.

5. Have a positive, energetic, excited attitude 100 percent of the time.

6. Live your life with integrity, faith, hard work, good honest values and believe in yourself!.

7. Take time to enjoy life's simple treasures. Travel, be adventurous, and have fun with family and friends!

When you follow this game plan, you are setting yourself up for a clear victory—win the game!

If you ask me how I want to be remembered, it is as a winner. You know what a winner is? A winner is somebody who has given his best effort, who has tried the hardest they possibly can, who has utilized

Chapter 25 – Summary

every ounce of energy and strength within them to accomplish something. It doesn't mean that they accomplished it or failed, it means that they've given it their best. That's a winner.

—Walter Payton

Chapter 26 – About the Author

Growing Up

I was born in Princeton, New Jersey, and lived there until I was eleven years old. I don't remember too much about Princeton. We had a basketball hoop in front of the house, and I did love to play basketball. It was always my favorite sport to play. I know I wasn't sad at all about leaving New Jersey and moving to Nahant, Massachusetts.

I believe that Nahant is one of the best places a kid can grow up. I was very fortunate to live and grow up there. I moved there when I was going into the fifth grade. Nahant is a peninsula, only about one mile square, with a population of about 3,600 people.

We had an awesome house right on the ocean. Our dad bought us a boat, a sixteen-foot, wooden lapstrake with a 1958 Johnson 35 hp engine, for $425.00. I absolutely loved working on the boat and enjoying it all summer long. I dreaded the fall when the boat had to come out of the water. Spring was the best—time to get the boat and the lobster traps ready for the season.

Fishing and lobstering was a fantastic hobby for me growing up. Bluefish, stripers, flounder, haddock, and cod were all around the island, and, boy, did I enjoy fishing. I had a student lobster license good for twenty-five traps, and my dad had a ten-trap license, so I would put out thirty-five lobster traps. I would haul the lobster traps two or three times per week and do pretty well. I loved eating lobster three or four times a week, and our family hosted awesome lobster bakes.

Chapter 26 – About The Author

Eventually, we upgraded the boat to a seventeen-foot fiberglass Seaway with a Yamaha 50 hp engine. A terrific fishing boat!

I attended Nahant Junior High through the ninth grade. I was the captain of the basketball team, and I was voted best athlete. I loved playing basketball and thought it was my best sport.

Just a side note—if I had known then what I know now about sport-specific training, I would have trained much harder and smarter. I would have researched extensively on how to develop my skills. This is a good message for kids in your teens: if you are good at a sport and you really enjoy playing it, do it with all your heart, and be the best according to your God-given abilities.

If you want to excel at a sport, it's so easy to search the Internet today to learn about any area you feel you could improve on:

- Speed and agility exercises

- Upper-body strength exercises

- Lower-body strength exercises

- Increasing core strength

- Increasing cardiovascular endurance

- Improving your jump shot

And then you need to have the self-discipline to make yourself practice and train in those areas to achieve your desired results.

OK, back to growing up.

Then I went to high school. There were no high schools in Nahant, so we had to pick between four high schools in Lynn. It was a big change from Nahant to Lynn. Let's just say that Lynn, Massachusetts, has a reputation of being a little hard-core.

I chose Lynn Classical and was very happy with that decision. I had a fantastic time in high school—what a blast. My buddies were Gary and Smitty, and we played football together.

I wouldn't say I was an outstanding football player; I held my own. Our team during my three years there was exceptional. We only lost three games in three years. We went to the North East Conference (NEC)Super Bowl twice, and we won it once. My dad cut out every article about our football games from the local paper and put them into a scrapbook for me. He was proud of me for playing football.

I played basketball my sophomore year, and I was riding the bench. They had a real good team, but a terrible coach. During a game, I watched one of the other players on the bench walk up to the coach and say, "Are you going to put me in, or what?" I said to myself, "This coach has no control over this team and isn't helping me improve at all." I stopped playing for the team at that point, a move I regret. I continued to play basketball in pickup games after school and park leagues for years. I would even skip class and sneak down to the gym to play.

I would not say Lynn Classical was the best academic school around; I don't recall ever bringing home a book or doing homework. I kid around with people and say the two things I learned at Lynn Classical were how to shoot hoops and roll joints.

I got kicked off the baseball team my sophomore year for shining a mooner out of the back of the bus. Don't ask me why I did that.

Chapter 26 – About The Author

I was voted best looking my senior year. So I guess that meant I was decent looking, which helped out in hooking up with girls. I went to the senior prom with a very beautiful girl. But I really didn't realize what I had, and I didn't really know how to treat a lady right. I hope she will forgive me for not being the gentleman I should have been. I probably still don't know how to treat a lady correctly, and that might be one of the reasons I am still single.

I really did have a fantastic time in high school.

The College Years

My dad was working at the University of Massachusetts Lowell when I got to college age, and it just made the most sense to go to that school. I selected mechanical engineering for my major and nearly flunked out my first year. As I mentioned, my high school was not that great academically. While all the other students in my calculus class had taken precalculus in their last year of high school, my school hadn't offered it. They actually ran out of math courses for me, and I took Algebra II review again. I had taken it my first year there and my last.

You need to have above a 1.4 grade point average to stay enrolled at the university, and I got a 1.406 my first semester. My dad got me a tutor for calculus, and I met a good friend, Doug, who taught me how to study.

My first year, I lived in the Smith Hall dorm. That was a lot of fun. My first weekend there, I heard a bunch of guys down in the corner room. So I walked down, introduced myself, and asked where I could get some beer. They said, "No problem. Toast is heading over to the package store shortly, and he will pick you up whatever you need." Toast was this guy's nickname because he was always toasted. And since he had had to stay back a few times, he was plenty old enough to buy alcohol.

I partied with those guys that night and throughout the next five years. We had a great crew. It was not a fraternity, but these guys called themselves the Bayzos. I am still not even sure what that means.

The College Years

We had an intramural flag football team, basketball team, volleyball team, and softball team, and we were very good. Playing on them was a blast. I can recall one very cold flag football game when my friend Pete, who was playing quarterback, had me run a quick out. I slipped and hit the ground, and when I looked up, the ball hit me right in the mouth. He had fired that ball. Boy, did that hurt. It was ice-cold out, and the ball was hard as a rock.

I got in a fight my first year at college. It was in the dorm; this guy down the hall gave me the middle finger with both hands for some reason. I chased him and caught him halfway up the stairs. We went at it in between floors. It basically turned into a wrestling match, and I believe I got the better of him. Anyway, the two residence advisors (RAs) had to break up the fight, and it drew a crowd. I can recall going to dinner the next night in the cafeteria and everyone looking at me and pointing me out. So that gave me a bit of a reputation of someone who liked to fight.

Now, I don't claim to be a tough guy, and I don't go looking for fights. One of the reasons I train hard six days a week is that if I need to defend myself or have to fight for something that is right, I will have the strength and endurance to get the job done to the best of my ability.

My second year at college was a beauty; I moved out of the dorm and got an apartment with five other guys. These five guys all knew each other and had played football at Haverhill High School. So they were big, strong, and a little crazy.

We would have the Bud representative drop off five kegs of beer every Friday night for a party. We would charge $3 at the door and make enough money to cover the rent, which was $550 per month. A fight would break out every party, and we would all jump on whoever started it and throw him out.

We destroyed that house and got evicted after the one-year lease was up—big surprise. That got us put on some type of blackball list for apartments in the area. We had to work hard to get another apartment.

Surprisingly enough, though, I got my best grade point average that year.

I was on the five-year plan. I would sign up for five classes each semester, and then I would drop the one class that I did the worst in or if I disliked the teacher. I changed my major after the first year to industrial technology. This was a combination of engineering courses and business management courses. It provided more options after graduation, and it was a little easier.

Those were crazy days. My roommates and I would occasionally flip over a car on our way home from a party or club. We would pick out a small vehicle in a parking lot, and then we'd all get on one side and flip it over. Why we did that, I have no idea. I apologize to anyone we did that to. It must have sucked coming out the next morning and finding your car flipped over. Tonto was missing in action for some periods during my college years. He would have advised me to act differently and to be smarter with some of my decisions.

One year, the college basketball team was having walk-on tryouts. Tonto was around this time, popped up on my shoulder and said, "What the heck, give it a try." I was the last guy cut from making the team. I was not discouraged; that actually wasn't bad for not having played for my high school team.

I met a great girl my second year at school, and we ended up together for about seven years. She was fantastic, and we had a lot of awesome times together. Why didn't we get married? Who knows? I guess I really like the freedom to go wherever I choose and do whatever I want. Perhaps I have commitment issues; I wasn't even sure how to spell the word. I am happy that she and I are still great friends, and we keep in touch. We can still get together for dinner and laugh and smile about the awesome memories that we created.

I worked three jobs while at college. I worked weekends at the Porthole Pub as a barback and bartender. I worked in the cafeteria for my dad, and I worked as a monitor at a study hall on campus. My dad, being the director of food service at the university, provided a free meal plan, and I paid for tuition, books, and housing myself.

The college years were terrific. I had a lot of fun, and I got that diploma!

My Bartending Career/Hobby

What did the grape say when the elephant stepped on it?
It didn't say anything; it just let out a little wine.

When I was eighteen and graduated from high school, I knew I needed to get a summer job to earn money to pay for college. Grandfather Gaudet lived across the street from us in Nahant, and next door to him was his son Paul. Paul's twin brother, Jay, owned and operated a large popular restaurant in Lynn called the Porthole Pub. I thought this would be a good place to work for the summer.

I remember seeing Jay and Paul lying out in the sun outside Paul's house. I thought it would be a good time to go and ask for a job. I was a little nervous, but Tonto appeared again and said, "What's the big deal? If he says no, he says no." So I went up and asked Jay for a job.

He said, "What can you do?"

I said, "Anything," and I told him I had worked for my dad in the food service business and catered parties.

He asked, "Can you operate a fryolator?"

I said, "I haven't used one, but I am sure I could learn."

My Bartending Career/hobby

He said, "OK, go down Monday afternoon and see my brother Bobby."

When I went in and saw Bobby, he had other plans for me. He had me trained to be a busboy and a barback. This turned out to be a very good job. I bused tables and barbacked there for the whole summer and made good money. I just saw Bobby last week, thirty-one years later, and we talked about the good old days.

When I started college in the fall, I still worked weekends at the restaurant. I worked every Saturday night busing tables and bar backing. I started at 5:30 p.m. and worked till 3:00 a.m. Then I came back in on Sunday and bused tables from 10:30 a.m. to 6:00 p.m. Working those two shifts, I always went back to school with at least two hundred dollars in my pocket, which was good money at that time.

Where is an elephant's sex organ?

In his feet, 'cause if he steps on you, you're fucked!

During the course of my bartending career, many jokes got told around the bars. If I heard a good one, I would write it down on a cocktail napkin and throw it into a shoebox where I saved silly things. I thought I would share some of those with you. I apologize if I offend anyone. And forgive me, Mom, for the swear words.

The bar backing shift on Saturday night was a fantastic job. It would get so busy, it would be four deep all the way around the bar. A line would form at the door around midnight, and it would end up being two hundred feet long. People would come from all over: Salem, Swampscott, Nahant, and all the other neighboring towns. Last call in those towns was 12:30 a.m., and at the Porthole it was 1:30 a.m. So all these people came to get a few more drinks, which most of them really didn't need!

The barback job consisted of keeping the beer coolers full, getting ice, filling the ice bins, filling the juice containers, and taking care of the glasses and empty bottles. Carrying three cases of beer through the busy crowd was challenging at times, but fun. I don't mind saying that I was really good at this job.

Being able to come out from behind the bar was great, because it allowed me to flirt with the girls, and there were plenty of them! And the cocktail waitresses were fantastic. There were four cocktail waitresses on Saturday night, and Jay hired the best-looking cocktail waitresses he could find. The waitresses would tip me out at the end of the night, so I would assist them with whatever they asked.

This grasshopper walks into a bar and jumps up on the barstool. The bartender comes over to him and says, "Hey, we got a drink named after you."

The grasshopper says, "Oh, yeah? You got a drink called Charlie?"

About the time I was becoming of legal age to drink, a lot of my friends would show up for last call. When it was four deep at the bar, some of my friends would yell to me, "Hey, Tom, grab me four Budweisers!" I wasn't supposed to, but I knew I could get them four beers, take their money, ring up the sale quickly, and return their change so fast that no one might see. It was very busy, and the other bartenders didn't mind, because it was helping them out. They were in the weeds. I believe the manager saw also and didn't seem to mind.

My Bartending Career/hobby

Then one night, we were all sitting around the bar—the cocktail waitresses, the bartenders, the doormen, and John, the manager. This was after all the customers were out and the cleaning was almost complete. John said to me, loud enough so the other bartenders could hear, "Hey, Tom, you have permission to fill in for any of these guys as a bartender if they need the night off." That was awesome. Getting a bartending shift at this very popular bar was not easy.

I was doing personal training at a gym when this beautiful girl walked in; she had an unbelievable body and was wearing some nice, tight spandex. This guy, one of our members, came up to me and said, "Which machine should I use that will really impress that chick"?

I said, "Try the ATM in the lobby."

I would then get calls to cover all the holidays and last-minute calls when they were stuck and needed someone. I didn't care; I was hungry for money. I would work any time I could. The guys would always trick me into working a holiday, like Mother's Day or Easter. They would ask me about six weeks in advance, "Hey, Tom, want to work a Sunday for me next month?" I would say sure. Then it would come around, I'd realize it was a holiday, and I would say, "Shit, they got me again…"

Mother's Day was the worst; you worked your ass off and made little money. I remember this one I worked with my friend Jay (not the owner, another Jay). We called it the Mother's Day massacre. It was busy as hell, with tons of kids and families who were not used to the bar scene. They didn't know how to order or tip correctly, and we were slammed—in the weeds for eight hours straight. We made about a thousand Shirley Temples. The money was weak that day, and we got our asses kicked.

I finally got my own shift, a Saturday night, which was fantastic. That was always a busy night. We had four bartenders on, and a fifth would come on at 11:00 p.m. to help with the rush. We took turns working "the Pit." The Pit was the service station at the end of the bar. You had to be real good to handle the Pit on a Saturday night. You had drink orders coming in from fourteen waitresses and had to wait on people on both sides of the Pit. I loved it, because it was so challenging. You would be flying, banging out drinks left and right from the waitresses and serving customers, and you could see and hear some people saying, "Wow, look at that guy go! He's good!"

The guys I worked with back then are still some of my best friends, even if I did have to carry them on Saturday nights. We had some real characters working there. One guy, who will remain nameless, was so funny. He would get to the point where he didn't want to wait on any more people, so he would fill a glass with ice and just walk up and down the bar like he was looking for a specific bottle of liquor. He would do this until he felt like waiting on someone again. You would see that same guy drinking a Coke all the time—or what looked like a Coke. we all knew it was half Burgundy and half Coke.

I worked at the Porthole for around twenty years. Then I was at a golf outing one weekend and ran into my high school friend Carl. He told me that they were looking for a bartender for Saturday night at the 466 Restaurant in Danvers, Massachusetts, where he was working. I was living in Danvers, and this restaurant was three and a half miles from my house—a lot closer than the Porthole, and the hours were better. This was worth looking into.

I went down to the 466 Restaurant to meet the owner, Richie, a great guy, and he decided to bring me on Saturday night.

My Bartending Career/hobby

My first night working there was a beauty. I did do some training prior to this shift with my friend Carl, but not too much. It was a very busy Saturday night, and I was on the bar with another guy named Jack. I thought, *This won't be bad; if I have any questions, I'll just ask Jack.* But before I could ask him a question, he started asking *me* questions. I didn't realize it was his first night working also, and he had never bartended before!

We made it through the night and laughed about it often. I did also pick up another shift on Thursdays with my friend Tim. Tim is a character; he specialized in socializing, jukebox playing, and flirting with the girls.

This restaurant, where I still work today, is a really cool place to work. It is a sports bar with excellent Italian food. The owners are awesome and are really good to work for.

I worked Thursday and Saturday nights there for five years before I moved to Florida.

> *This elephant got a thorn stuck in his foot, and it was giving him great pain. He saw this ant, and he said to the ant, "Hey, you're supposed to be able to lift ten times your weight. If you pull this thorn out, I'll do anything for you." So the ant went over, gave a real hard pull, and the thorn came out. The elephant was amazed and relieved. He said, "Thank you so much! Name it—what can I do for you?"*
>
> *The ant said, "How about letting me fuck you in the ass?"*
>
> *The elephant kind of chuckled and then said, "Sure, if that's what you want." So the ant climbed up the*

back of the elephant and started going to town. Meanwhile, up in a tree there was this monkey watching the whole thing go on. The monkey started hurling coconuts at the elephant's head. You could hear the elephant moaning, "Ouch, damn! Wow, my head!"

Then all you heard was that ant yell out, "That's right, bitch! Take it all!"

While I was down in Florida, I got a part-time bartending job at a Marriott Hotel in Fort Lauderdale. This was a neat job. I ran a small bar in the lobby and also took care of room service. At first, I wasn't crazy about this room service thing. But then I realized each check had a 20 percent gratuity fee included, so that was a 20 percent tip guaranteed every time. So when the phone rang at my small bar, they might order two or three entrees with drinks. I went back to the kitchen and gave the order to the chef. When the food was ready, I brought it up with the drinks. I greeted whoever answered the door with a high-energy, positive attitude and a smile, and they usually tipped me on top of the 20 percent.

I worked a six-hour shift 4:00 p.m. to 10:00 p.m. on Saturday and Sunday nights. Getting done at 10:00 p.m. on Saturday nights down in Fort Lauderdale was terrific. It left plenty of time to go enjoy the nightlife. The bars stay open till 3:00 a.m.

The chef would make me whatever I wanted for dinner. There was a big TV back in the kitchen/dining area. This area was open for breakfast and closed in the evenings. If it was slow on a Sunday evening, the chef would make us up a big appetizer platter, and we would kick back and enjoy the NFL games on that TV. I did that job for around a year, until I left Florida.

My Bartending Career/Hobby

When I got back to the Boston area, I was extremely fortunate to pick up a shift at the 466 Restaurant, where I had worked before. I picked up Wednesday night and eventually every other Friday night. Wednesday night is a great shift. I am the only bartender on, and I work with Joyce, a really cool manager, and we have a lot of fun.

Friday nights, I work with my buddy Carl. Carl and I went to high school together, and we have a blast reminiscing and laughing about our high school days. We go back and forth between hockey and basketball—which is the better sport, which has the better athletes. He played hockey, and I loved basketball.

Once in a while, he throws a check into me while we're working to try to prove a point that hockey players are tougher. As a matter of fact, he throws so many checks that I have to work only every other Friday just to let my body heal.

I have had a part-time bartending job since I was eighteen. I think it is one of the best part-time jobs you can have. The money I earn bartending pays for my food, gas for my car, and my spending money for the week. My check from my full-time job pays all my other bills. It works out really well.

There was a very short time when I gave up the bartending. I quickly realized that it is much easier to get a girl's phone number on the inside of the bar instead of the outside…

My Manufacturing/Engineering/Production Career

I graduated from college with a bachelor of science degree in industrial technology in 1987. My first job was with UPS in New York City at 643 West Forty-Third Street. I was hired by the industrial engineering department, and I started off driving a truck to learn the operation. Driving a UPS truck in Manhattan was a unique and fun experience. Something crazy would happen every day, like having to step over a body bag to deliver a package, or having the prostitutes wave to me in the morning on Forty-Second Street.

One day, I was driving my UPS truck and stopped at a red light. I looked over, and on the corner, dressed in a nice three-piece suit, was my friend Craig whom I grew up with in Nahant. Craig had a very high-end job in New York City at the time. I yelled over, "Craig, is that you?"

He ran up to the truck and said, "Wow! What a cool job you have! Can I jump on and help you deliver a few packages?" He stayed on my truck for the rest of the day. He didn't go back to work, and we had a blast.

I actually loved New York City, but the cost to live there was ridiculous. I had to live in New Jersey, and the commute in and out of the city was awful and expensive. I would get up for work at 6:00 a.m. and not get home until 9:00 p.m. The money was very good, but not enough to pay all my bills and student loans.

In between graduation and starting this job, I did have a few other interviews. There was one job I was very interested in: a manufacturing

My Manufacturing/Engineering/Production Career

supervisor position for Philips Lighting Company, located in Lynn, Massachusetts. They told me a position was going to open up soon because one of the other supervisors was going out for a knee operation. I kept in touch with the human resources manager at Philips while I was working in New York. About four months into the UPS job, when it started getting cold and I was still out delivering packages, I said, "That's it. I am heading home." I pulled over my UPS truck and called that HR manager at Philips. I said, "I will be home in two weeks and would love that manufacturing supervisor's position." Sure enough, I got the job.

It was a third-shift position, which had its challenges. But it was a very good job with a very good company. They had great benefits and were located about three miles from my parents' house in Nahant. I moved back into my old room and went from not keeping up with the bills to putting away a thousand dollars a month.

The third-shift job was pretty cool in the summer. I would get home about 7:00 a.m., have a bite to eat, and head out in the boat. I would go fishing and lobstering until about 2:00 p.m., head home, eat again, sleep, and get up for work at 9:00 p.m.

The job was challenging. As I mentioned in chapter 10, I was in charge of running two production lines: unit twenty-four and unit twenty-five. Each line had twenty-four employees and produced fluorescent light bulbs at a rate of forty per minute. There was a production schedule to adhere to, which included changeovers for different customers. This was a union shop, so any disciplinary actions had to be handled with the union steward present.

I can recall the mechanic on one of the production lines, named Joe. He was fifty-three years old. He did not like taking direction from a twenty-three-year-old kid just out of college. It took about six months for him to realize that I wasn't a bad guy and had a pretty good head on my shoulders. And we became good friends.

There were two accomplishments that I was proud of at Philips. The first was when the company decided to start up a third shift in their compact fluorescent PL department; it was only running a first and second shift at that time. They asked me to hire all the people needed to run the third shift, including a mechanic. I interviewed, hired, and trained the entire third shift. The expectations throughout the company were that we would start off at around a 70 percent efficiency rating, compared to the 93 percent efficiency rating on the first and second shifts, and that it would take us months to get up to the higher level. Well, the training went so well that the first week we started up, we were in the nineties! Eliminating the shutdown and start-up each day improved the overall efficiency of the department. In just a few weeks, all three shifts were operating at around a 96 percent efficiency rating, which was awesome.

The other accomplishment that I thought was really cool happened in our packaging department. Because our production line was running twenty-four hours a day, we had to shut it down for a three-hour window in the middle of the week to get some preventive maintenance done.

During this time, the people would move over to our hand-packing operation. They had to take twenty-watt fluorescent light bulbs out of a tote, put a protective sleeve over each one, put six in a case, and tape them up. Well, the industrial engineer at the company calculated that we should have so many cases done in that three-hour window, and I was not coming close to that number. My boss was telling me I needed to improve the output of those people, and I was only coming in at 60 percent attainment to schedule. I could not understand why this wasn't working. I watched closely everyone working all the time. I went to the industrial engineer and basically said, "I think your calculations are wrong and that our target is too high." He proved to me that the calculations were correct and that there was sufficient time to meet the required target.

My Manufacturing/Engineering/Production Career

So, I came up with a new idea. I had eighteen people in that department, so I took the target cases for the shift and divided it by the number of people to determine the exact amount each person would have to pack to be at 100 percent. I rearranged the packing operation so that all workers would have their own stations. I put the exact amount of light bulbs at each station. I told them, "When you finish packing the bulbs at your station, you can have the rest of the shift off. I can recall one girl—Phan was her name—who was a great worker; she would fly. She got hers done in one and a half hours and would have one and a half hours off. End result: I went from 60 percent to 100 percent basically overnight.

It was funny—the first-shift supervisor would come in and see everyone on break and say, "What the heck is going on here?" When I told him what I had done and that we hit 100 percent, he was impressed.

I had spent almost three years at this company when they made the announcement that they were shutting down the plant and relocating/consolidating the production lines with other Philips locations. Some of the production lines went to North Carolina, some went to Kansas, and the line I was working on moved to Juarez, Mexico. The labor costs were the big reason for this move. You see, we were paying our workers around $11.00 per hour, and in Mexico, the workers would be paid $0.98 per hour, which was a big difference.

I collected unemployment, worked as a bartender, and did landscaping work while I looked for another job.

After around two months, I got three job offers at the same time:

- Third-shift injection molding supervisor at a plastics company in Newbury, Massachusetts

- First-shift manufacturing supervisor at a car parts company in Waltham, Massachusetts

- Second-shift production supervisor at Gorton's of Gloucester

All were good positions. I had had enough of third shift; the sleep schedule was not normal. So the plastics company was out. The commute to Waltham in the mornings on Route 128 would have been awful, so that job was out. Gorton's had an excellent benefits package and a very good reputation as an employer; it had been in business since 1849.

I had an outstanding fifteen-year career at Gorton's, and it turned out to be an excellent choice. I held the following positions:

- Second-shift production supervisor

- Process engineer

- Third-shift production manager

- Production manager for all three shifts

- Schichtleiter (shift leader)—Bremerhaven, Germany (sister company)

- Back to production manager

- Plant operations manager

These positions were indeed challenging. I learned a lot working at Gorton's and met many excellent people. It was a union environment, and there was plenty of pressure put on us to hit production goals.

My Manufacturing/engineering/production Career

The highlight of my career at Gorton had to be my two years in Bremerhaven, Germany. I can recall vividly the day the vice president asked me to consider this opportunity. He pulled me aside after a meeting and said he needed to talk to me in private. Immediately, I thought I had done something wrong. He said, "We have a sister company called Frozen Fish International, located in Bremerhaven, Germany. I have spoken to the director of this company, and we came up with the idea to swap a production manager at each facility so that we can learn best practices from each other. This would be a two- to three-year assignment." He said, "I know this is a big decision, and you will probably need a few days to talk with your family before making it."

I looked at him and said, "This sounds like a fantastic opportunity. I don't need any time to make this decision. I'm in!" This was my gut instinct and Tonto just said you are a fool if you don't jump on this assignment!

I did have to fly over for an interview to make sure the people in Germany approved. This was quite the trip. My brother and our girlfriends at the time brought me to the airport. There was an engine problem with the plane as soon as it was fully boarded, and they made us all get off the plane. We had to wait for the next one. I called my brother, and he came back to the airport with the girls so they could all hang with me until the next plane was ready. It ended up taking five hours, and a number of beverages were consumed in that time frame.

Finally I got on the plane. I sat in nice, comfortable first-class seats; these first-class tickets had cost $4,000 with Lufthansa. The first thing the flight attended said was, "Champagne or beer?" I went with the champagne. It was a six-hour flight to Frankfurt, where I needed to switch planes and get on one to Bremen. Since my first flight was five hours late, I missed the second flight I was supposed to be on and had to wait another four hours for the next plane at that airport. Being in first class allowed me nice privileges in the first-class lounge, including a complimentary bar. Like I needed more beer. I finally arrived in Bremen, and then I had a one-hour taxi drive to Bremerhaven.

After about twenty-two hours of traveling and drinking, I made it to my hotel room. I was exhausted. I put my bags down and lay on the bed. As soon as I shut my eyes, the phone rang. It was the production manger and a process engineer. They were in the hotel lobby, ready to pick me up and start the interview. They had not known about the first plane problem that had delayed everything. I told them, "At least let me jump in the shower, and I'll be down in twenty minutes."

When I got down there, they were at the hotel bar having a beer; they said, "Would you like one?"

I said, "Why not?" Then we had an excellent dinner at the hotel with a bottle of wine. It was a fantastic hotel, and this trip and interview seemed like one long, fun party. The next day, I went to see the company, and I must have made a good impression, because they all agreed to the project.

Now, I must admit, I was a little nervous getting on that plane the next time, knowing it was a one-way plane ticket. I did not really know anyone over there, and I did not know what I was in for. It was more of an excited, nervous feeling. Tonto reassured me it was the right call. He said, "Sometimes in life, we have to take chances, and this would be a rewarding one."

One month prior to my departure, I took a Berlitz immersion course in German. That was fun: going into Boston, meeting with a female teacher for three hours in the morning and then with a male teacher for three hours in the afternoon. The woman was tough; she didn't let me speak any English. She was from Germany and had only lived in the United States for one year. The guy teacher was easier; he was from the United States and had only spent a few years over in Germany.

My Manufacturing/Engineering/production Career

My First Day of Work in Germany

Oh my God, this was quite the day. I recall going into the HR office and meeting the secretary, Christiane. She was great. She greeted me with a smile and spoke English. Christiane and her husband, Carlo, turned out to be my best friends over there, and we are still great friends today. Then she introduced me to the HR manager, Herr Karch. He greeted me in German and just started rambling on in German for what seemed like ten minutes. He then stopped, looked at me, and said to me in English, "You did not understand anything I just said, correct?"

I said, "Yes, correct. I did not understand what you were saying." I could tell he was disappointed with my knowledge of the German language right off the bat. I had studied it in Boston for one month, but that was clearly not much. Over in Northern Germany, they spoke a lot faster and in a different dialect.

Herr Karch thought for a moment and then said to my counterpart (their production manager, who was training me), "No one is to speak English with Mr. Muser. He must learn this language." And that became law. For the rest of that day, which went for ten hours, I tried as best as I could to understand what all these people were saying to me. My head was ready to explode, and I wondered if I had made the right choice. I asked Tonto what he thought. He said, "You can't quit after just one day. You must work at least one more day." So I went back to my hotel and to the bar in the lobby, and I spoke my first German sentence: "*Ich möchte gern ein Beck's vom Fass, bitte.*" (I would love a draft Beck's, please.) I would go on to work there for two years, and it was a fantastic experience.

When I returned from Germany, I went back to the production manager position at Gorton's. I was responsible for all three shifts, and the people really welcomed me back and were happy to see me. I was able to apply some of the best practices that I had learned in Germany, and I continued to make improvements and meet the production schedule for the next two years.

At that point, the company decided to do some organizational changes. Big companies like to do this occasionally to shake things up, remotivate people, and avoid any complacency.

I moved from production manager to plant operations manager. I was responsible for five departments that had a total budget of $2.1 million. I thought, *Do they really want to put me in charge of spending $2.1 million?*

The five departments I was responsible for were:

- Waste Removal

- Warehouse and Material Transportation

- Cafeteria

- Plant Security

- Uniforms

This was a challenging position and an excellent learning opportunity. There were a few highlights I experienced during this stage in my career:

I switched from the uniform company we had been working with for years. This was no easy task. All 185 employees needed to be measured for their new uniforms. And then, in one weekend, the old uniform company came in and took out their lockers and all their uniforms. Then the new company came in and installed all new lockers with the

My Manufacturing/Engineering/Production Career

new uniforms inside. This project went through without a hitch, and the result was better-quality uniforms, better customer service, and $75,000 yearly savings. This was not a one-time savings. Each year, the company saved that $75,000.

Upgrading the security cameras and digital recording system was another nice improvement project I was able to complete. We had an old recording system with videotapes. We added more cameras to cover every exit and entrance and had the software and recording equipment connected to our desktop PCs to be able to look at any situation at any time. This was a huge improvement.

Also in the security department, I was in charge of securing an inner and outer perimeter of the plant. You see, this was after 9/11, and everyone learned to be very aware of what terrorists could do. They might even try to contaminate large food companies. This project involved making picture IDs for each employee. They had to swipe their cards, which had magnetic strips, to get into the inner perimeter of the plant. This was a fun and successful project that improved the security of the facility.

With the warehouse and waste removal, there were many lean-thinking projects that I was involved with. I learned a lot about lean thinking, value stream mapping, and kanban systems (these use signs and signals to increase production efficiency). A lot of these lean manufacturing principles originated in Japan. I am thankful for these experiences, because what I learned with these principles can be applied to many areas of life.

I was in that plant operation position for two years, and it was a terrific experience.

Then something happened to me. I started watching people around me retire, and many people who were just counting the years till retirement. I attended some funerals for people who had worked at the company for thirty-five and forty years. Soon after their retirements, they passed away. To be honest with you, this scared me. Tonto even had his doubts. He said to me, "Is this all there is to life? You work all these years at a company, retire, and die? Don't you want more?"

My Personal Training Career

When I was in my last year at Gorton's, I was taking a kickboxing class taught by my friend Tommy. I went to high school with Tommy, and we always will be good friends. He is a three-time world-champion kickboxer. He is an extremely talented and dangerous person. I really enjoyed his class and learned a lot. Tommy got very busy with his real estate investments and other life matters and was not able to make some of his kickboxing classes. He asked me to fill in and teach them. He was also preparing for his next fight and asked for my help with some of his training for it.

This was an incredible experience and really taught me what serious training was all about. The condition you need to be in to fight professionally is amazing. Tommy's expertise was in cardiovascular conditioning. He told me he won a lot of his fights just by having more wind than his opponent. His opponent would get tired quicker, and then it was all over for him.

Let me share with you one of his training routines. We went to the track at Salem High School. He would run the track, a quarter mile, and then sprint the last straightaway. At the end of the straightaway, I would be waiting, wearing a double chest protector and focus mitts. I would hit the timer for a three-minute round, and then he would throw combinations of kicks and punches and basically beat the hell out of me for three minutes. At the end of the three minutes, he would run the track again, sprint the straightaway, and do another three-minute round of punching and kicking. He would do this for twelve rounds.

The fight he was preparing for had two-minute rounds with two-minute rests in between them. He trained for three-minute rounds and ran a quarter mile for his rest. Do you think he was in better condition than his opponent?

After one of these sessions, he said to me, "You know, you are really good at this—training people. You should do it for a living." That gave me the idea of being a personal trainer. I absolutely loved the gym, and after that, the thought of the gym floor being my office just consumed me.

I got my first personal training certification from the International Sports Science Association. Studying for its exam was awesome, because in the past I had done so much studying and taken so many courses on topics that I was not excited about. It was such a cool relief to study and learn about a subject I was passionate about.

I was still working at Gorton's at this time, and all I kept thinking about was being a personal trainer and learning more about the human body and how it worked. I felt that I had to plan for a career change.

This was an extremely bold and risky move. Some people might say it was a stupid move. I was on track to make around $108,000 that year in salary and bonus. I had earned five weeks paid vacation and twelve paid holidays. I had great medical, dental, and life insurance. And I was vested in the pension and had a 401k with generous matching.

Tonto and I sat down and went through the decision-making exercise I outlined in chapter 21. It wasn't even close. An overwhelming number of positive bullet points were in favor of making the change.

I knew I needed to save up some money prior to this move. I knew I would need to build a client base and that it could take some time. I planned to do the move in March so I would get my tax refund and a company bonus to add to my current savings. I had $25,000 in savings prior to the move.

I did some basic math; I said I could earn $50,000 doing personal training, $25,000 bartending, and $25,000 from my vacation rental business, which added up to $100,000 per year. I was a single guy with no kids; I decided $100,000 per year was plenty of money to live on.

I wrote my letter of resignation and brought it into my boss's office on a Monday morning. He was surprised. I recall him saying, "You know I'm going to try to talk you out of this." After he heard my plan and could see the excitement I had to start a career in personal training, though, he realized I had my mind made up.

I shared this with you earlier: Confucius said, "If you work at what you love to do, you never have to work a day in your life." So I really considered this a type of retirement, and I felt that I didn't have to work anymore. "Plus," Tonto said to me, "if you can be very successful in a field that you don't really have a passion for, how successful can you be in a field that you have an incredible passion for?"

I got the first personal training job I interviewed for; it was at a Gold's Gym in Salisbury, Massachusetts. First, I interviewed with the fitness manager, and then I sat with the fitness manager and general manager. I can recall the general manager saying to me in the interview, "Can I be so bold as to offer you the position on the spot? I can tell you are what we are looking for." At this time, this facility was the third-largest Gold's Gym in the world. It was seventy-five thousand square feet, with over six thousand members.

I remember all too vividly my first paycheck—I have already mentioned that it was only $20.00. I earned $20.00 per session and had trained one person that week. I had gone from earning $51.92 per hour to $20.00 per week. I was not discouraged and was not going to let the situation affect my attitude and drive. I was determined to succeed. I will not lie to you, though; I struggled for the next four months and got up to earning around $310 per week doing about ten sessions each. We did receive a 10 percent commission for selling a PT package, so it went up from $20 per session to about $31 per session.

The owner of this Gold's Gym also owned four others, so we had a regional fitness manager who supported all the clubs. He would hold a monthly meeting at one of the Gyms, and all the personal trainers attended—around thirty-five per meeting. He gave out prize money to the top three personal trainers. First place in personal training sales would get $100, second place was $75, and third place was $50. This was not a lot of money; however, I wanted to get into the top three. I wanted to be called up there in front of this group and be recognized as one of the best. The manager handed out a sheet of paper, nothing fancy, and it listed all thirty-five personal trainers in the order of their personal training sales. When I first got this piece of paper, I did not like seeing my name toward the bottom of the list. I said to myself, "I want to be in the top three."

It was August, and I had been at this new career for four months; my savings of $25,000 was nearly gone. I had made this career change with four mortgage payments and a lot of bills. I thought, *Perhaps this really was not a smart move, and I should go back into the manufacturing/production world where I can get a higher, steady paycheck.*

Then my regional fitness manager said something that stuck. "What if failure was not an option?"

Tonto said to me, "What if you had to succeed at this profession? What if your life depended on it? What if you did not have the option of going back into manufacturing?"

My Personal Training Career

So I put my head to the grindstone (I have no idea what that means—sounds like it would hurt). In other words, I went to work. I found out what was holding me back and limiting my paycheck.

When I sat down with a potential client for the complimentary hour, I would say, "I would love to work with you. Here are our options for personal training packages."

What do you think happened? Ninety percent of potential clients would say, "I would love to do personal training with you, but I just cannot afford it at this time."

And I would say, "OK, I understand. If things should change with your financial situation, please let me know." Then the person would leave, and I would not see him or her again.

What changed was that I needed money to put gas in my car and food in my fridge and to pay the bills! So when the prospect said to me, "I don't have the money," I could truly relate. But I knew some of these people *did* have the money, based on their profession and some other key indicators. They were just spending it in other areas that seemed to them to be more beneficial at the time. For most of these people, I knew that investing in their health was a much better option. So when I heard "No, can't afford it at this time," I would say something like this: "I realize money can be tight; however, I can teach you things that are going to benefit you for the rest of your life. These things could add five or ten years to your life. What's that worth?" I would say things like, "You put money into your car to maintain it—oil changes, new tires, and preventive maintenance. How long do you plan on owning your car—three or five years? How about your body? How long do you plan on owning that? Are you trading it in after three years? Well, if you are not trading it in, it might make sense to put some money into it so it lasts longer." I did not accept no easily, and I convinced people that my training was a smart investment in their health.

I started getting clients left and right. Other members saw me getting busy and wanted in on the action. By September, I had tripled my paycheck; I went from earning $300 per week to $900 per week. The next month, at the regional personal trainer meeting, I was in the top three. I would be one of the top personal trainers in the company for the next year, and I was training thirty to thirty-five clients per week.

After almost two years at Gold's, I wanted to get to the next level. This was a terrific job, and I was having a blast. But I had reached the highest pay level for personal training, and the benefits were not that good, like no paid vacations. A friend of mine, Melanie, told me about opportunities at the Boston Sports Clubs; a corporation called Town Sports International (TSI) runs them, with a total of 153 clubs. They offered a higher rate of pay and good benefits. I sent Melanie my résumé, and she gave it to Rob, the fitness manager there at the time.

I interviewed with Rob at the South End Boston Sports Club, and although the opportunity was very good, the commute would not work for me. Rob forwarded my résumé to the Lynnfield Boston Sports Club, and I went there for an interview. I met with Nick, the fitness manager, and got the job. Nick and Rob are still great friends of mine. They are both very knowledgeable about the fitness industry; I learned a lot from them.

I was there only a few weeks before the general manager pulled me aside and asked me about my career goals. She presented an opportunity of a fitness manager position at the Lexington Boston Sports Club. It seemed like a great opportunity, so I interviewed for it and got the job. This was another awesome experience; I had a fantastic two years at the Lexington Boston Sports Club.

I remember my first day there. I walked in, and the group exercise coordinator approached me at the front desk, introduced herself, and asked, "Can you teach a total-body conditioning class?"

My Personal Training Career

I said, "Sure, I can do that." The former fitness manager was supposed to be there to train me and to teach that class, but he decided never to show up again. I taught the class, and it went great. I continued to teach it for the next two years, growing the attendance from fifteen to thirty-five people per class.

We had a fantastic team there in Lexington; we set records for the highest month ever in personal training revenue and personal training sales. The general manager, Dan, and the group exercise coordinator, Kristy, are both truly gifted in their field. And when you work with talented people, you can make some great things happen. As the fitness manager, at that time, I got a bonus when I hit a monthly target for personal training sales and personal training revenue. That was a potential of twenty-four bonuses per year added to my base salary and training. That year, I hit twenty-three out of twenty-four possible bonuses—not bad.

After two years there, I got an offer from my brother Andy and his wife Kim that I could not turn down. They were living in Coral Springs, Florida, right outside Fort Lauderdale. They had a beautiful, four-bedroom house with a swimming pool in a great neighborhood. It was just them and their dog living there. They kept telling me, "Hey, Tom, we got this empty bedroom with your name on it. We know you love Fort Lauderdale, and you can do personal training and bartending down here!"

Finally, I had enough of the cold New England winters, and I decided to take them up on this offer. This was another risky move. I gave my notice to two excellent jobs: fitness manager at the BSC in Lexington and two shifts at the 466 Restaurant. And I had no job lined up in Florida and four mortgage payments. Was I nuts?

Well, after I gave my notice at those two jobs, I quickly started looking for jobs online in Florida. I found one that was perfect: fitness director at a gym called Fitness 21. I sent a nice cover letter along with my résumé and got a call to set up a phone interview. I had three phone interviews, and they decided to fly me down for an interview in person. And I actually got that job before I stopped working in Massachusetts.

I drove down to Florida on a Wednesday, got there Friday night, and started work at Fitness 21 the following Monday.

This was a fantastic job: a beautiful, twenty-five-thousand-square-foot facility loaded with plenty of body building equipment. Here's a photo of Fitness 21:

I was in charge of a talented team of twelve personal trainers, and I had a blast working with them and growing the business.

The gym was doing around $22,000 per month in personal training revenue when I arrived. And we were able to get that up to $40,000 per month. This was a great accomplishment that I am proud of. I worked for Phil Kaplan at this time. I consider him a very good friend and mentor. I learned so much from Phil, and I will always be grateful for that opportunity.

I remember my first week there. A man came up to me and was looking for a refund for his remaining personal training session. I said to him, "You can use that session with another personal trainer here at the gym or with me." The personal trainer he had been working with had recently left the company, around the same time as the previous fitness director.

The man said to me, "You lost your two best personal trainers here at the gym; I would just like my money back."

I said to him, "Just let me take you through a workout at no cost. After the workout, if you still want the refund, I will process that." It took a little more convincing, but eventually, he agreed.

I took him through the workout, and he loved it. He ended up training with me once a week. Then his wife started training with me also. And then his son joined in too! That was a nice success. You can read his wife Jo-Ann's testimonial toward the back of the book.

It was interesting to see the different styles of personal training between Boston and Florida. I absolutely loved working at that gym and living in Coral Springs.

Three months after I arrived, the company my brother Andy was working for started to have some trouble and laying people off. They offered him a nice severance package, and he was back in the job market. He could not find anything in the Florida area, but he finally landed a really good job in Denver, Colorado. That put me in a little bit of a predicament. One of the reasons I had moved down there was to spend time with my relatives. Also, living at their house was affordable, considering I still had the mortgage payments up north.

I had just built up my clientele to the point of making a decent paycheck, and that had been a lot of work. I decided I could not move back to Boston then, and I started looking for an apartment. I found a fantastic condo for rent right off Fort Lauderdale Beach. It was about five hundred yards from the beach and had a nice swimming pool. It was only $800 per month.

There was a condo association, so they had to have me sit in on a meeting with the board to vote on letting me rent there. Before the meeting, one of the board members said to the person in charge, "Hey, you're not going to let that kid move in here, are you?" He had seen me taking a tour of the complex a few days earlier. I guess I looked young; I took it as a compliment.

The head guy said to him, "He's no kid; he is in his forties."

They let me in! It was a terrific spot, located between Las Olas Boulevard and Sunrise Boulevard. There were easily twenty-five great restaurants and bars all within walking distance. It was under a mile to Hooters on Fort Lauderdale Beach—one of my favorites.

This was really amazing, because at that time, if I could have picked any place in the world to live, it was Fort Lauderdale Beach. And if I could pick any job to have while living there, it would be the fitness director position I had where I could also do personal training. There are not too many people who could have said that. That situation lasted thirteen months.

Then came another important decision in my life. My mom had been battling cancer for seven years at this point. Then came her fifth operation, which involved removing her voice box. It was incredibly frustrating to try to communicate on the phone with her after that. She still wasn't cancer free and had to be taken to radiation and chemotherapy treatments weekly. I knew it would not be long before the good Lord would take her up to heaven.

Even though I was really enjoying myself in Florida, I kept thinking I was going to eventually get the call to come home for my mom's funeral. I hated that. I knew the right thing to do was to head home and spend some quality time with her before she went. Also, my brothers Marty and Dan were helping out big-time by taking her to all her appointments and being there for support. Tonto appeared and said, "Tom, you should be home, helping out the family! It's time to go home and do your part!"

So I made the decision to move back to the Boston area. First I let my landlord know; he needed thirty days' notice. Next, I had to tell Phil, and I was planning on giving the gym three weeks' notice.

I called Phil and said that I needed to talk to him. I met him at an LA Fitness Gym in Boca Raton. It was near his house, and we planned on working out there also. This was tough; I told him in between sets on the hammer-strength lat pull-down machine. I could tell he was disappointed, because he was happy with my performance and things were going well. When he heard the circumstances, though, he could relate. His parents were around the same age, and he totally understood.

Next, I gave the Marriott my two weeks' notice. I had been working at the hotel part time on the weekends as a bartender.

I few days later, I woke up in the middle of the night in a cold sweat. I was freaking out. I got up and paced the floor in the living room. I was saying to myself, "Are you freaking crazy? You just gave your notice on your dream job, you just gave up this terrific apartment, you don't have a job up there, and you still have four mortgage payments and all sorts of other bills to pay. How are you going to pay them all?"

You see, I had made the mistake earlier that night of looking on the Internet to see what kinds of jobs were available in Massachusetts. I had come across an article that said unemployment was the highest it had been in twenty-six years. This was in 2010.

So I kept pacing the floor and talking to Tonto. "You can't just keep giving your notice on great jobs; you are eventually going to get burned. You don't have some magical gold horseshoe up your ass that's going to save you all the time…"

So I did what I usually do when I am worried about something: exercise. I dropped to the floor there in my living room at 3:00 a.m. and did as many push-ups as I could till failure. Then I did another set, and another. I ended up doing ten sets of push-ups, close to five hundred reps, and then I went to bed.

People talk about having anxiety and depression; I truly believe the best medication on the planet for those is exercise. I can be worried about something and go get a great workout. After the workout, I'll say, "I can't believe I was worried about that."

So I enjoyed my last week in Florida. I did get in some beach time and bar-hopping. I have a strict rule that I do not date any of my personal training clients; it is more professional that way. But since I had stopped working at the gym, they were no longer my clients. A few of them wanted to meet me for a drink, which was awesome. I never quite figured this out, but when girls know that you are moving far away, they want to sleep with you. Why is that? I really should just move somewhere new every year; I might get more action.

I sold my furniture on Craigslist and made enough for the gas money to get home and hotel rooms along the way. The night before I left, I did see a fitness services manager position at the Boston Sports Club in Lynnfield listed on CareerBuilder.com. This health club was located eight miles from my parents' apartment, and I had actually worked there before for a very short time.

As I was driving home, I made a call to my friend Nick who worked at the company and asked him about the position. He suggested I call the district manager of the region to express my interest. I knew the district manager; when I worked at the Lexington Boston Sports Club, he was their regional district manager.

So I called him on my way home; I believe I was in North Carolina. We played phone tag back and forth, but I finally got to discuss the position with him. I think I was in Virginia at this time. This was a Tuesday, and we set up an interview for Friday. I met with him and then met with the general manager of the Lynnfield Boston Sports Club. I got the job.

That night, I dropped into the 466 Restaurant where I used to work. I wanted to see some of the people and also find out if there were any bartending shifts available. It just so happened that one of the regular part-time bartenders had stopped working there a few months earlier, and the guys had been rotating the Wednesday-night shift. The guys all had full-time jobs as well, and although they liked the extra money, it was a little demanding on their time. The owner asked me if I would like to work that shift. I said I would love to and thanked him.

So, unemployment was the highest it had been in twenty-six years, and I drove home to Boston and within one week had two jobs. How does that happen? My dad teaching me the importance of a strong work ethic, that's how! Both of these employers knew who they were getting. I had worked for them for years. I was punctual and professional; I never called in sick; my appearance was in order; and when I was there, I worked all the time.

So now I was able to spend some time with my mother and father. I ended up getting an apartment right next door to them for a few months, and that was great. I would walk over with my coffee in the morning, sit with my mom, and just chat. I was home for nine months, and then the Good Lord decided to bring her up to heaven.

One of the things my mom loved to do was read. Every three weeks, I would bring her to the library in Danvers, and she loved it. She would always take out eight books and read them all within the three-week period. I wasn't much of a reader when I started bringing her to the library; I would usually take out one book and not even read half of it. One time, I finished a whole book in the three-week period and could not wait to tell my mom I had done that. Yeah, it was a book on anatomy, and it was mostly pictures. But what the heck; I finished it. It made me realize I could read in my field and become better at what I do, so I started reading more and more.

I think Mom would be very proud to know that I am writing this book. It is one of the reasons I am writing it. I plan on donating a portion of its proceeds toward cancer research in honor of my mom. I want to raise a lot of money toward that cause so people won't need to suffer like she did. When this book becomes a success and does its part toward curing a terrible disease, I think my mom will look down on us and smile.

Three weeks after my mom passed, my dad had a diabetic stroke. I believe it was caused by the lost of our mom; they had been married for fifty-three years. He is now in a nursing home and doing OK. I've mentioned that he has dementia and has trouble communicating at times. But we can still get a smile and a hug from him, and he still recognizes us!

My Personal Training Career

I plan on staying in this area until my dad decides to join my mom up in heaven, and I am in no rush. I really enjoy visiting him and having a cup of coffee with him. I also have more family up here that I can spend time with.

I am still working at the BSC in Lynnfield today. I am not the fitness services manager any more. I am a full-time master trainer.

The fitness services manager position changed to include different requirements and responsibilities; the role turned into more of a sales position. The job is to meet with all new members, explain the fitness products available, and recommend the best product for their goals. The company did not want the fitness manager to do any personal training. But personal training is why I got into this industry; it is the fun part of the job. So it was not hard for me to choose full-time master trainer over the new fitness manager role.

Now I am able to work my own schedule. I work Monday through Friday—only half a day on Friday—and this is awesome. I leave work early on Wednesday to go to my bartending shift, and I start my day at noon on Thursday. Fridays I am done by 3:00 p.m. and can head to Cape Cod or up to the White Mountains of New Hampshire. And I have weekends off to work on my rental properties. I have many special clients, and I really look forward to going into work. This setup also allows me to spend more time with my dad.

One thing is for sure: I am not going to go to my grave and say, "I always wanted to be a personal trainer but never was." Not only did I go out and become one, I have had a ten-year career as a trainer so far. Not many people can say they get to wear shorts and sneakers to work. And how many people can say they can't wait to get to work and really love hanging out on the gym floor all day, taking care of business and making a living?

Thomas Edward Muser

Don't aim for success if you want it; just do what you love and believe in, and it will come naturally.

—David Frost

Chapter 27—Deleted Scenes

(My nieces and nephews are not permitted to read this section; it could alter their opinion of Uncle Tom.)

White Russians

When I was twenty-one years old, I was playing in a softball league in Nahant. The team I played for was the Knights of Columbus. After the games, the whole team would go down to the Knights hall to drink some beer, play some pool, and talk about the game.

One night, we went down there after a game and started off with a round of beers. I got myself a Heineken. Then my friend Chuck grabbed me for a pool partner. I recall him saying, "Let's play for White Russians." We won the first game, and the losers brought us over a couple of large White Russians in mugs.

Now, I am really a beer drinker, but I said, "What the heck. I'll try it," and it went down pretty good. Well, we kept on playing pool and kept on winning. And the White Russians kept on coming. We played for hours.

When we left the Knights, I had the not-so-bright idea of driving one of my friends home, across town to the other side of Nahant. Well, I wasn't driving that well and hit a curb. My front hubcap went flying off and ended up on the third-hole green on the golf course.

The blue flashing lights soon appeared behind me, and the cops pulled me over. I did not do well with the sobriety tests and spent the night in jail. When I walked home from jail in the morning, I stopped by the third-hole green and picked up my hubcap.

I got myself a good lawyer and decided to fight the case in court, because that's what people told me to do.

I was nervous as hell on court day. When it was my turn to go up on the stand, the district attorney was scary and tried to break me down. I told him that I only had one Heineken. He kept asking me, over and over again, "Are you *sure* you only had *one beer*?"

And I could say with confidence, "Yes, sir, I only had one beer!"

I was found not guilty. I remember saying to my friends outside the courthouse, "I'm sure glad he didn't ask me how many White Russians I had!"

Two in the Loft

I was bartending one Sunday at the Porthole Pub; the shift was 11:00 a.m. to 7:00 p.m. When I got done with work, I decided to stick around and have a beer or two.

This girl I knew and her friend decided to join me for beverages. They were both very attractive. For some reason, we decided to do some shots—Slippery Nipples (Sambuca and Bailey's), if I recall correctly.

It was karaoke night, and there was a pretty good crowd for a Sunday night. This restaurant is pretty big and has a seating capacity of around two hundred. The upper loft area seats around thirty people.

As the night went on, I noticed the upper loft area was empty. I thought, *What if I could get the two girls up there for some privacy?* They were open to the idea, and we snuck up there with some beverages. One thing led to another, and clothes started coming off. We were all getting naked, fooling around, and having a grand old time.

We thought no one could see us! Apparently, the DJ running the karaoke show had a pretty good view. He was not amused, and he recognized me. He decided to call the owner the next day and let him know what one of his bartenders had been up to.

The next day, I got the phone call from the owner. He asked if it was me up there in the loft with two girls getting naked and fooling around. I could not tell a lie and said, "Yes, it was me."

He said, "I am going to need to suspend you for one week. Do not come into work next week, and don't let this happen again." I had never been suspended from work or received any type of disciplinary action at any of my jobs. I was really embarrassed to tell anyone I got suspended.

About a year later, I was hanging out with the owner, having a few beverages and he said to me, "You know, Tom, when I got that call from the DJ and he told me the story, I didn't know whether to fire you or give you a raise!"

A $3,500 Night

One Saturday, when I was living in Germany, I woke up and felt like driving to Brussels, Belgium. It was about a five-hour drive from where I was living in Bremerhaven, and I had always wanted to visit the city.

I usually do some research on the places that I travel to; however, in this case I did not. Research is a good idea, especially currency exchange rates. When I pulled over to fill my gas tank in Belgium, it cost thirty-three hundred Belgian francs. This was before the Euro was in place. So I really did not do the conversion in my head; I just thought there were a lot of francs in a dollar. I was too excited about exploring this new country.

I arrived in Brussels and drove down the center of the city and picked out a beautiful hotel right in the middle of the city. Again, it cost many Belgian francs for the room. The room was awesome, and the bathroom had its own phone and marble throughout.

So I showered up, put on some nice clothes, and went out to hit the town. In the lobby, I asked them where a nice restaurant was. Fortunately, they spoke English and directed me to a great restaurant. There are three languages spoken in Belgium: Dutch (the version spoken in Belgium is sometimes referred to as Flemish), French, and German.

This restaurant had one of the biggest buffets I had ever seen. It had many types of excellent seafood, steaks, and chicken. It was a protein bonanza! I got myself a nice bottle of wine and ate and drank like a king for the next few hours.

I headed out on the town again. I found this club down the road with live music and plenty of people dancing and having a good time. I hung out there for a few hours, drinking. I experimented with all the different types of Belgian beers, and there were many of them.

I didn't hook up with a girl at that establishment, so it was off to the next one. I hopped in a taxi, and the driver asked where I wanted to go. I said, "Somewhere with a lot of girls."

He brought me to this place, so I walked in. A girl came right up to me and said, "Follow me." I liked this place already! She brought me to a room where, to my surprise, girls were lined up against the back wall. She said to me, "Pick one." I thought that buffet earlier in the night was good…but I think I liked this one better!

I saw this gorgeous Brazilian-looking girl, so I said, "I like that one."

My hostess said, "That is a nice choice; however, she does not speak any English or German. Might I suggest the blonde over here? She speaks very good English."

I replied, "Can I have both?"

She said, "Sure!" Of course, a credit card had to be handed over at this point.

The two girls took me to a large, private back room. It had its own dance floor with a stripper's pole in the middle. A waitress came in to take our drink order; one of the girls wanted a nice bottle of champagne. Go figure—it was delicious.

The girls danced for me while I sipped champagne, just enjoying life.

A $3,500 Night

Then I said to them, "My turn. You both sit down and relax, and I'll dance for you." Don't ask me why, and please don't repeat this, but I was actually wearing a G-string, along with my cowboy boots. I got up on the stage and put on a show for them. They both applauded with big smiles.

We fooled around, drank, danced, and had a blast for the next three to four hours.

Finally, the gentleman from the front of the house came back, handed me my credit card, and said, "Sorry, sir, but this card has been maxed out." It was time to leave. I gave each girl a kiss and was on my way.

When I walked out of the establishment, to my surprise, it was light out. I took a taxi back to the hotel; it was about 8:00 a.m. This hotel was set up with a breakfast area in the lobby. It was full with everyone having breakfast as I walked through. Everyone seemed to stop eating and stare at me. I guess I looked like I had been out all night.

I went up to my room, slept for about four hours, checked out, and then drove back to Bremerhaven.

When I got my credit card statement, I totaled up the cost for my one night in Brussels—$3,500.

Testimonials

With the help of Tom, I have lost five pounds of fat and gained four pounds of muscle in just six weeks! He's given me a great variety of exercises so I never get bored, and he inspires me to challenge myself every time I'm at the gym. It's comforting to know that I have a trainer as serious about my fitness goals as I am. Thanks, Tom!

—Amanda DeLoof

I started with Tom about a month ago and I am already seeing results that were so hard to achieve on my own. I am twenty-five years old and have been working out and playing sports my whole life. I never thought about working with a personal trainer until now. I highly recommend Tom for anyone who is serious about getting results. He knows what he is talking about, and he keeps the workouts fun, creative, and focused. Thanks, Tom!

—Gabriel Shapanka

Tom Muser is a very knowledgeable, experienced trainer who is able to assess your needs, develop a program to help you achieve your goals, and provide fun exercises that will challenge and help improve you. I was exercising on my own but not losing weight or achieving the body strength or tone I desired. Through Tom's guidance

Testimonials

and expertise, in just seven weeks I was able to lose ten pounds, strengthen muscles, improve posture, strengthen core and balance, and generally improve physical and mental outlook along with gaining more energy. He is extremely pleasant and always supportive of my efforts. I give Tom a five-star rating and will definitely recommend him as a trainer.

—Linda Anderson

Dear Tom, I wanted to take the opportunity to let you know how well the fitness program is going. In just these first thirty days, I have gone down one pant size, lost five pounds, and gained some muscle mass. But apart from the physical changes, I am also feeling mentally more alert and aware. I dare describe it as elation and a feeling of well-being. I feel it both at home and at work, and others have noticed the changes as well. Thanks for your support and for being a trainer that listens to what we want to accomplish and helps set realistic goals for us. You designed a program that works within my abilities yet challenges them at the same time. I will gladly recommend you to my friends and family.

—Laz Amador

Despite our differences in politics and sports teams, Tom has done a superb job of getting me back in shape! I was overweight, I used to feel tired all the time, plus my back was bothering me. Thanks to Tom's training regimen, I have gained five pounds of muscle, and I feel much better! I am very satisfied with Tom's workouts, and I will continue seeing him for many years to come!

—Christian Montenegro

Thomas Edward Muser

There are a multitude of reasons why people don't go to the gym. For my son and me the number one reason was the equipment and the whole idea of going intimidated us. At the urging of my husband, he talked us into working with a personal trainer: Tom Muser.

From the first day, Tom treated us with respect and, most importantly, patience. He spoke of "synergy" and how the three parts of successful training come together:

1. Proper eating

2. Cardio training

3. Weight training

But we think one more should be added to this list. For a complete synergy approach to work, Tom Muser is an integral part. We value his patience and attention to detail as he carefully explains each machine's purpose and demonstrates correct lifting techniques. He is always aware of personal limitations, but still encourages us to push through to the next level.

Our successes have been tremendous, and Tom has been with us all the way. He sets the goal just within reach when trying your best and pushing yourself to the limit. Fat loss and muscle gain are the results. Thank you!

—Jo-Ann Mathes

There is no way I would ever push myself as much as Tom pushes me during my training sessions. He is really the manager of my "psych."

—Stephen Dionne, USPTA Tennis Teaching Professional

Testimonials

Three years ago, before I started working out with Tom, I went to the gym and exercised without results. Going to the gym was a chore and not something that I really looked forward to. That has all changed.

I expected the beginning to be about form and more lifting weights. Boy, was I wrong! Tom takes a holistic approach, looking at lifestyle, diet, and medications, and then he tailored a program to meet my needs and maximize results. At first I was very skeptical, but Tom's positive high energy and easygoing manner motivate me to keep trying.

Are there observable benefits? Absolutely. My high blood pressure condition has been mitigated, my doctor is amazed, and my attitude in and out of the gym has changed to be much more positive and less stressed. I sleep better, and my alcohol consumption has dropped considerably, as I know it will affect my workouts the next day. People who see me can't believe my age and usually think I am ten years younger than I am.

Working out with Tom has been life changing. Any regrets? Only that I did not start working out with Tom sooner!

—James Ryan

Appendix A

Sample Weekly Shopping List

This list is for one person weighing 175 pounds targeting a 2,500-calorie-per-day nutrition plan. Adjust accordingly.

Carbohydrates

Item	Quantity	Ounces	Cost
Whole-Grain Pasta	2 boxes	26.5	$1.78
Whole Wheat Bread	1 loaf	24	$2.50
Bananas	5	27	$0.78
Apples	5	13	$1.92
Carrots	1 bag	16	$1.49
Broccoli	1 bag	12	$1.19
String Beans	1 bag	12	$1.19
Cherry Tomatoes	1 carton	12	$1.67
Cucumbers	3	7	$0.89

Protein

Item	Quantity	Ounces	Cost
Tuna	3 cans	15	$5.00
Chicken Breast	4 lbs	64	$12.00
Top Round Steak	2 lbs	32	$6.58
Salmon	1 lb	16	$5.99
Lean Ham (low sodium)	1 lb	16	$3.29
Skim Milk	1 gal	16	$2.49
Eggs	1 dozen	21	$1.99

Fat

Item	Quantity	oz	Cost
Almonds	1 bag	12	$3.49
Extra Virgin Olive Oil	sm bottle	5.7	$2.99

Weekly Total = **$57.23**
Total per day = **$8.18**

Note: These are actual food prices at Market Basket in Danvers, Massachusetts

Appendix A

Substitutions:

Ezekiel Bread for whole wheat bread
Brown rice for pasta
Any fruit for any fruit
Any vegetable for any vegetable
Lean protein for lean protein
Good fats for good fats

Appendix B

Weekly shopping list broken down by macronutrients and some micronutrients

Carbohydrates

Item	Quantity	Ounces	Calories	Protein	Carbs	Fat	Saturated Fat	Sugar	Fiber	Sodium (mg)	Cost
Pasta (WG)	2 boxes	26.5	2800	98	574	21	0	28	84	140	$1.78
Bread (WW)	1 loaf	24.0	1600	80	304	32	0	48	48	2880	$2.50
Bananas	5	26.7	525	5	135	0	0	70	15	5	$0.78
Apples	5	12.8	475	0	125	0	0	38	8	4	$1.92
Carrots	1 bag	16.0	175	5	40	0	0	25	10	325	$1.49
Broccoli	1 bag	12.0	100	8	16	0	0	4	8	80	$1.19
String Beans	1 bag	12.0	100	4	16	0	0	8	8	40	$1.19
Tomatoes	1 carton	12.0	240	12	76	4	0	20	4	40	$1.67
Cucumbers	3	7.1	72	2	12	0	0	6	2	8	$0.89
Carbs Subtotal =		149	6087	214	1298	57	0	247	187	3522	**$13.41**
Per day =		21	870	31	185	8	0	35	27	503	

Protein

Item	Quantity	Ounces	Calories	Protein	Carbs	Fat	Saturated Fat	Sugar	Fiber	Sodium (mg)	Cost
Tuna	3 cans	15.0	360	90	0	4	0	0	0	1360	$5.00
Chx Breast	4 lbs	64.0	1920	416	0	24	8	0	0	1200	$12.00
Steak	2 lbs	32.0	1520	200	0	72	28	0	0	520	$6.58
Salmon	1 lb	16.0	917.5	97.5	0	55	10	0	0	273	$5.99
Ham	1 lb	16.0	800	100	8	9.5	3.8	7.6	0	3341	$3.29
Skim Milk	1 gal	16.0	1440	128	208	0	0	192	0	2080	$2.49
Eggs	1 dozen	21.2	852	72	0	60	24	0	0	840	$1.99
Protein Subtotal =		180	7810	1104	216	225	74	200	0	9613	**$37.34**
Per day =		26	1116	158	31	32	11	29	0	1373	

Appendix B

Fat

Item	Quantity	Ounces	Calories	Protein	Carbs	Fat	Saturated Fat	Sugar	Fiber	Sodium (mg)	Cost
Almonds	1 bag	12.0	1980	66	66	187	16.5	22	33	0	$3.49
Olive Oil	sm bottle	5.7	1320	0	0	154	22	0	0	0	$2.99
Fat Subtotal =		18	3300	66	66	341	39	22	33	0	**$6.48**
Per day =		3	471	9	9	49	6	3	5	0	

		Ounces	Calories	Protein	Carbs	Fat	Saturated Fat	Sugar	Fiber	Sodium (mg)	Cost
Weekly Total =		347	17197	1384	1580	623	112	469	220	13135	**$57.23**
Total per day =		50	**2457**	**198**	**226**	**89**	**16**	**67**	**31**	**1876**	**$8.18**
Calories per day =				791	903	800	144	268	126		
Percentages =				32%	37%	33%	6%	11%	5%		
Daily Requirements (per USDA and Harvard School of Public Health) =								50	35	2400	

Appendix C

Tracking: Budget 2013

Spending	May Budget	May Actual	Difference
US Bank: Danvers Mortgage	$1,970	$1,970	($0)
Bank of America: Home Equity Line	$611	$611	$0
Bank of America: Credit Card	$0	$0	$0
Danvers Natural gas	$154	$127	$27
Danvers Electric	$60	$63	($3)
Danvers Comcast Cable and Internet	$50	$78	($28)
Danvers Water/Sewer	$88	$148	($59)
Danvers House Maintenance Costs	$0	$0	$0
Chase: Credit Card	$0	$0	$0
Verizon: Cell Phone	$100	$90	$10
Brookline Bank: Auto Loan	$0	$0	$0
Food	$282	$328	($47)
Beer/Wine	$40	$14	$26
Auto Insurance and Maintenance	$0	$103	($103)
Gasoline for Auto	$175	$242	($67)
Entertainment/Social	$100	$300	($200)
Church	$12		$8

Appendix C

Gifts (Birthdays, anniversaries, etc.)	$20	$210	($190)
Education - Personal Training	$0	$0	$0
Haircut	$0	$19	($19)
Health Care	$0	$0	
GMAC Bank: Isalene Mortgage	$1,777	$1,777	$0
Isalene Natural Gas	$65	$36	$29
Isalene NSTAR Electric	$25	$17	$8
Isalene Comcast Cable and Internet	$13	$123	($110)
Capital One: Equity Line	$243	$244	($1)
Isalene Hyannis Water System	$25	$0	$25
Isalene Verizon: House Phone	$0	$0	$0
Isalene House Maintenance Costs	$0	$528	($528)
Rental Business Expense	$0	$624	($624)
Isalene Trash Pickup			$0
Chase Bank: St. Joseph Mortgage	$1,196	$1,231	($35)
St. Joseph Hyannis Water System			$0
St Joseph House Maintenance Costs	$50	$0	$50
New Hampshire Taxes			
Total	**$7,053**	**$8,882**	**($1,829)**
Yearly =	$84,633	$106,585	
Gross Pay Needed (28% deductions) =	$115,935	$146,006	
Income			
Personal Training		$2,604	
Rental Properties		$3,000	
Bartending		$1,564	
Total Income =		**$7,168**	
Difference =		**($1,714)**	

235

Writing this book has been an incredible experience for me. It has helped me realize the things I need to focus on moving forward to get the absolute most out of life.

I thank you very much for reading this book! I hope you got a lot out of it and that it helps you improve the quality of your life.

If you have learned something from this book or if it has impacted your life in a positive way, please feel free to share your story. You can send me an e-mail at thomas.muser@yahoo.com. Also, please feel free to visit my website: tommuser.com

Resources and Recommended Learning Tools

Books

Roger Earle and Thomas Baechle, *NSCA's Essentials of Personal Training* (2004).

Dr. Frederick Hatfield, *Fitness: The Complete Guide*, 7th ed. (2001).

Paul Insel, Don Ross, Kimberly McMahon, and Melissa Bernstein, *Nutrition,* 4th ed. (2011).

National Academy of Sports Nutrition, *Optimum Performance Training for the Health and Fitness Professional*, 2nd ed. (2004).

Courses:

Dr. Anthony Abbott, *Exercise Science Foundations Course*, Fitness Institute International

Websites

National Library of Medicine—National Institutes of Health
www.nlm.nih.gov

Resources And Recommended Learning Tools

Centers for Disease Control and Prevention
www.cdc.gov

Phil Kaplan's Fitness and Weight Loss Solutions
www.philkaplan.com/

Audio Programs

Earl Nightingale, *Lead the Field*

Brian Tracy, *The New Psychology of Achievement*

John Cummuta, *Transforming Debt into Wealth*

For additional audio programs, I recommend:

Nightingale-Conant
www.nightingale.com

Author Biography

I currently work full time as a master trainer at the Boston Sports Club in Lynnfield, Massachusetts. In addition to being a personal trainer, I consider myself a life coach, nutrition consultant, teacher, educator, and mentor to others. I have sixteen different certifications in the fitness and nutrition field. My goal is to help people improve the quality of their lives through positive lifestyle changes.

I also work part time as a bartender and have done so for over twenty-five years. I believe bartending is one of the best part-time jobs you can have.

Prior to working as a personal trainer, which I have done for ten years, I worked in the manufacturing/engineering world. I have a BS in industrial engineering with a minor in computer science. I had a terrific eighteen-year career in that field, working as a production supervisor, process engineer, production manager, and plant operations manager.

Out of this unusual combination of education and experience, along with entertaining, real-life stories, I created this book to help energize, motivate, and entertain people.

I currently live in the Boston, Massachusetts, area. I am single and have never been married. My fantastic mom is up in heaven; my terrific dad is hanging in there; and I have four cool brothers, one sweet sister, three great sisters-in-law, and seven awesome nieces and nephews.

Made in the USA
Middletown, DE
19 June 2015